PENNSYLVANIA
MOUNTAIN
LANDMARKS

Pennsylvania Mountain Landmarks

VOLUME 1

Jeffrey R. Frazier

an imprint of Sunbury Press, Inc.
Mechanicsburg, PA USA

an imprint of Sunbury Press, Inc.
Mechanicsburg, PA USA

Copyright © 2023 by Jeffrey R. Frazier.
Cover Copyright © 2023 by Sunbury Press, Inc.

Sunbury Press supports copyright. Copyright fuels creativity, encourages diverse voices, promotes free speech, and creates a vibrant culture. Thank you for buying an authorized edition of this book and for complying with copyright laws. Except for the quotation of short passages for the purpose of criticism and review, no part of this publication may be reproduced, scanned, or distributed in any form without permission. You are supporting writers and allowing Sunbury Press to continue to publish books for every reader. For information contact Sunbury Press, Inc., Subsidiary Rights Dept., PO Box 548, Boiling Springs, PA 17007 USA or legal@sunburypress.com.

For information about special discounts for bulk purchases, please contact Sunbury Press Orders Dept. at (855) 338-8359 or orders@sunburypress.com.

To request one of our authors for speaking engagements or book signings, please contact Sunbury Press Publicity Dept. at publicity@sunburypress.com.

FIRST CATAMOUNT PRESS EDITION: April 2023

Set in Adobe Garamond | Interior design by Crystal Devine | Cover by Lawrence Knorr | Edited by Lawrence Knorr.

Publisher's Cataloging-in-Publication Data
Names: Frazier, Jeffrey R., author.
Title: Pennsylvania mountain landmarks volume 1 / Jeffrey R. Frazier.
Description: First trade paperback edition. | Mechanicsburg, PA : Catamount Press, 2023.
Summary: Pennsylvania hikers know how rugged our mountain trails can be, but also how alluring they are; often causing us to wonder just what's around the next bend in the path. This volume offers some answers, providing an armchair journey to some of the most unusual and inaccessible landmarks that can be found in the mountains of Pennsylvania.
Identifiers: ISBN : 979-8-88819-130-9 (paperback) | ISBN : 979-8-88819-131-6 (ePub).
Subjects: NATURE / Ecosystems & Habitats / Mountains | HISTORY / United States / State & Local / Middle Atlantic (DC, DE, MD, NJ, NY, PA) | SPORTS & RECREATION / Hiking.

Product of the United States of America
0 1 1 2 3 5 8 13 21 34 55

Continue the Enlightenment!

CONTENTS

Acknowledgments		vii
Introduction		1
1.	The King's Stool (Dauphin County)	5
2.	Stairways to the Stars (Berks et al.)	10
3.	Umbrella Rock (Elk County)	19
4.	The Three Sisters (Huntingdon County)	25
5.	Lewis' Rock (Cumberland County)	34
6.	Infernal Evidence (Clearfield et al.)	42
7.	*Memento Mori* (Jefferson et al.)	55
8.	Picture Rocks (Lycoming County)	69
9.	Boxcar Rocks (Lebanon County)	76
10.	Warriors' Mark (Huntingdon County)	80
11.	Vampire Rock (Clinton County)	86
12.	More of the Same (multiple counties)	94
Bibliography		108
About the Author		109

ACKNOWLEDGMENTS

I want to acknowledge my appreciation for the help I've received from friends and guides who shared their knowledge and photographs as I wrote this book. Their help has been invaluable in leading me to and providing details about the many places featured herein. The hikes to these spots are experiences I will never forget. As my current lady's father once said, after gazing upon the hazy blue mountain peaks of central Pennsylvania that surrounded his farm, "mountains are good places to rest the eyes!"

It is a sentiment with which I heartily concur, but I also find that when the Pennsylvania mountains call to me somberly, I must go to them! Passing by sun-dappled woods, peering down into a dark hollow and wondering what secrets it hides, or watching clouds shroud a mountain peak, are sights I cannot resist, and fortunately, I have many friends who feel the same way.

I have been on many hikes with hiking groups over the years and continue to do so. I've also hired several guides to take me to spots I would have been hard-pressed to find. It is to those folks to which I dedicate this volume, but I also want to acknowledge the respect I have for those who have the same passion and commitment to save Pennsylvania's natural heritage as those who did so in the late nineteenth and early twentieth century. May their efforts bear fruit; otherwise, I fear we'll not get a second chance.

THE LOST TREASURES OF YORE
(A lament written by the author following the death of his first wife)

Give me woods to walk in or give me a hill to climb
Show me a stream to sit by, where I can pass the time

Let me rest on a mountain, and listen to the leaves
As they softly chatter in a gentle summer breeze

A valley to look down upon as wispy clouds float by,
their smoky tendrils caressing a deep blue azure sky

No matter if the weather is sunny or if the sky is grey
Here on this lofty mountain is where I hope to stay

I'll listen to the peepers and the raindrops' gentle sound
As they kiss the laurel, and patter on the ground

The smell of the woods will fill my head,
And keep me happy until I once again tread

Back to the valley, far, far below,
Where from which I departed, long, long ago

And now the night wind is calling me home,
Back from the mountains on which I once roamed

So I leave the hills and valleys of yore
And go back to the cares of life once more

The old wisdom was truth in so many ways
Of that, I am sure, as I count my days

The mountains will stand as long as there are men,
But once you've gone, you can't go home again

INTRODUCTION

In my many travels, I have been fortunate to have been abroad three times; to Japan, Germany, and France. When in France, I enjoyed a cruise up the Seine River while admiring ruins of medieval castles and ancient villas crumbling along the riverside. On land, I spent three weeks walking the avenues of Paris, Honfleur, Le Havre, and the streets of many quaint French villages. I also reverently strolled along the beaches of Normandy and explored the mysterious places featured in *The Da Vinci Code,* that compelling film about the messages supposedly hidden in the paintings of Leonardo DaVinci.

In Germany, I spent three weeks visiting sites along the Rhine River from Frankfort to the Black Forest, leisurely stopping at any tourist attraction or castle site that held some appeal. Those places included an ascent up to the Drachenfels, where ancient Celtic mythology says Roland slew a dragon, bathed in its blood, and became invincible.

Likewise, I climbed up a steep flight of stone steps into Frankenstein Castle, the very place that inspired Mary Shelley to write her chilling novel *Frankenstein,* the famous monster in her novel of the same name that was created there. Much to my surprise and delight, the castle, and the winding dirt road leading up to it, still look the same as they do in the original black and white movie based on Shelley's novel.

And I shall never forget walking along the ramparts of the castles at Heidelberg and Marksburg, visiting the witch museum at Rudesheim Am Rhein, looking down upon the statue of the Lorelei in the Rhine River north of Oberwesel, and gazing upon the *Siebengeberge* or Seven Hills of the Rhine.

But despite the colorful and enduring impressions those spots and adventures imprinted upon my mind, they nonetheless have not exceeded, or in some cases have not even matched, the scenic natural wonders I've found in Pennsylvania, especially those that are highlighted in this book.

I seem to have an unquenchable desire to explore the mountains of Pennsylvania. In the years I've spent researching and locating every spot featured herein, and I've visited almost all of them except for several where I could not get permission from the property owner to do so, I have climbed up to many mountaintops, touched the "roof of Pennsylvania," and seen the glory of the world below.

I have stood under the waterfalls of Round Island Run in Sproul State Forest, dared to enter the Devil's Dining Room at Bilger's Rocks and explored the labyrinthine passages there, climbed the Indian Steps and the Thousand Steps, twisted my way around the Standing Stones of Rocky Ridge, looked down upon Ticklish Rock, and rested under the shadow of Umbrella Rock.

I've even ridden in an original Conestoga wagon, pulled by a team of sturdy Belgians, to explore the depths of Pennsylvania's so-called Grand Canyon, being awed by the towering peaks on both sides and seeing the cliff of the wailing child, celebrated in the legends of the area's Native Americans who are said to have avoided it like the plague.

I've taken pictures of these unusual spots and found human-interest stories and legends clinging to these places that seem as old as the rocks. Quite often, I've also found that these unique and appealing spots, and their tales, are steeped in the spiritual charm of the Native Americans and imbued with the pioneering spirit of the Pennsylvania wilderness as it existed when the earliest settlers penetrated its dark interior. Such qualities led me to deem it a worthy effort to help preserve them all for posterity, and so you, the reader, will be regaled by these same tales and historical accounts in this volume and two future volumes of *Pennsylvania Mountain Landmarks*.

Become acquainted with a cascading boulder field said to have been dumped there by the devil himself and with an infamous outlaw whose hideouts included multiple caves and labyrinthine passageways among the rocks of eastern Pennsylvania. Such are the tales of which legends are made and which add color and mystique to the mountains, forming their very soul. This breath of life, hints of a less complicated and more compelling past, appeals to me and has inspired me to seek it out; to find the spots where it still survives, and bask in the local color and lore that surround them.

To preserve those accounts, which may otherwise have been forgotten in the decades to come, became one of my objectives when writing this book. But I did so with some trepidation knowing how true scholars in history and folklore are reluctant to put any credence in oral traditions and undocumented folktales because they often seem so unbelievable.

This dismissal, however, leaves an open field for an untrained non-scholar like me to search for any kernels of truth that may lie behind the tales, and I've attempted to do just that in some of the accounts that cling to the landmarks heralded in the chapters that follow and in my *Pennsylvania Fireside Tales* series containing many more accounts of the same kind.

But preserving the stories surrounding the landmarks was not the only motivation for this book. I was also inspired when I looked back to the first decades of the twentieth century. During that age of Progressivism, far-sighted men like President Theodore Roosevelt, Joseph Trimble Rothrock, Pennsylvania's first State Forester, and Gifford Pinchot, the Keystone State's conservation-minded governor, championed the preservation of our forests for the common good.

By instilling an appreciation for our natural heritage in the people of the Commonwealth, these men, and those of like minds, successfully saved our woodlands. And when regarding our present political environment, it seems apparent that a re-instilment of that appreciation is sorely needed today.

Financial and business interests are once more threatening nature's delicate balance worldwide. And if we don't find a way to counteract climate change's devastating effects, we may once again find our mountains reduced to barren hills, similar to those left by early lumbering interests who sacrificed an arboreal paradise for dollars. Entrepreneurs who, in exchange for millions of board feet of timber, callously and shortsightedly left behind nothing more than thousands of acres of bare slopes and shattered stumps.

So by sharing pictures of the marvelous places that can still be found in our forests and by recalling the quaint tales of human interest, adventure, and historic novelty that add zest to them, I hope this book will prove to be some small help in combatting climate change. Perhaps, by convincing enough people that it is a task worthy of their consideration, it will, in some small way, increase support for the current efforts, which are the only hope we have of saving our planet.

If I ever am given credit for preserving the folktales and legends of Pennsylvania and if I have inspired others to save the earth, then let that be my reward. I have been rewarded enough by being able to collect and preserve Pennsylvania's legendary culture, and none too soon. Mankind's numbers continue to grow, and our encroachment upon the natural environment is the worse for it, as is our cultural heritage.

It is highly doubtful that there are any places left in our state where life has not been affected by the modern world, with its Internet, cell phones, and cable television. If so, then the places where the old stories and legends could once be heard are scarce, except perhaps for some of the places highlighted in this book.

For, as J. F. Campbell in his *Popular Tales of the West Highlands*, that renowned classic collection of Scottish folklore, has said, "But as there are quiet spots in the world where driftwood accumulates undisturbed, so there are quiet spots where popular tales flourish in peace because no man has interfered with them."

CHAPTER 1

THE KING'S STOOL

In the Northern Ireland County of Derry, near the ancient lake called Lough Foyle and somewhere high up in the Binevenagh Mountains, there is a massive pile of rocks that, when viewed head-on, look like a large throne—so large that it could serve as a seat for a giant, or at least for a large person of great importance. Locals consequently dubbed it "The King's Stool," and it takes its place among the many remarkable landmarks of the Emerald Isle.

It was so remarkable that when Irish immigrants came to settle in Dauphin County, Pennsylvania and found a similar rock bench on Short Mountain in the Kittochtinny Hills, they were inspired to give it the same name. In so doing, they perhaps felt a little closer to the land from which they had come, and it must have also given them a sense of kinship with the land on which they now lived.

There is no record of fairytale-type legends associated with the King's Stool of Ireland, nor any of that type that is recalled about its Dauphin County cousin. However, the monarch's seat in Pennsylvania does have a remarkable story about it that was once well-known and frequently recalled by the residents of Clark's Valley who lived in its shadow.

Among the earliest settlers in that idyllic place was a German immigrant named Ludwig Minsker, who settled there with his family in 1750. It was a time when the Pennsylvania frontier was plagued by the Indian troubles of the French and Indian War, and Minsker and his neighbors were always on the lookout for marauding Indian war parties.

Minkser family tradition recalls that during this period, their ancestor, alarmed by a report that local rangers on Short Mountain had spotted an Indian war party, hid his wife and six-month-old son in a large wooden chest into which he drilled air holes for them. Here they remained hidden, the father supplying them with food and water until the danger passed.

It is said that this very same chest, with its air holes, has survived to the present day and is cherished as a colorful family heirloom by Ludwig's descendants. However, the tale does not end there. The young child hidden in the chest was also named Ludwig, and he grew up and raised his children in the same valley, just below the magnificent natural landmark that has weathered the test of time into the present century.

From this second Ludwig Minsker, the most well-known story of Dauphin County's King's Stool originated. Like the rocks it celebrates, the tale somehow managed to survive the ravages of time; seemingly floating undeterred on time's currents until it ultimately found a safe harbor in the place where the events it recalls occurred.

During this particular episode, the Indian troubles here had subsided, and the remaining Native Americans in Clark's Valley had settled into a peaceful coexistence with their white neighbors. Nonetheless, there were still some "Indian haters" who held grudges against them.

So one morning, when Mrs. Minsker had stepped outside their cabin door, she was alarmed by what sounded like screams of agony. Her husband dismissed them as the cry of a "painter," one of the common names used to refer to mountain lions in those days, which could still be seen and heard throughout the state at that time.

The incident was forgotten until some days later when the Minsker children, who had been sent out to look for the family's errant cows, the herd having failed to come back to the barn at their usual time, came running back home to excitedly report a grisly discovery they had made at the King's Stool.

They had managed to track the missing cows up to the top of Short Mountain, where they finally stopped to rest at the King's Stool. Twilight was slowly turning to darkness when they spotted a body at the foot of the unique jumble of rocks. The flesh had long rotted away, leaving only a skeleton of bleached white bones dressed in distinctive garb. They initially

A View of the King's Stool on Third Mountain.

On the King's Stool (My late wife sitting on the giant throne).

wanted to investigate further, but lengthening shadows spurred the frightened children to turn and run home to tell their parents about their macabre find.

The next day the children showed their parents the bones that lay at the foot of the rocks. The clothing the person wore at the time of his death, including a colorful hunting shirt, was recognizable as that often worn by a friendly aborigine who lived in a small hut on nearby Peters Mountain. But how he came to be here and why someone would have wanted to kill him was a mystery to the Minskers.[1]

Whether the Minskers ever discovered an answer to that mystery is unknown, but they probably did so at some point since they were undoubtedly told the same story that was told to me one April day in 1991. My storyteller, an eighty-two-year-old gentleman who was a lifelong resident of Clark's Valley and a direct descendant of Ludwig Minsker, had been told the story by his father.

This account claimed that the murder victim, known to locals as "Indian Joe," was killed by outlaw Indians when he attempted to prevent them from kidnapping the wife of Indian trader Peter Allen, whose trading post and house were located on the mountain named for him; Peter's Mountain. Allen's beautiful stone house still stands there today and is used as a private residence.[2]

The story of the Indian's demise is a longer tale, and it can be found in its entirety in the author's *Pennsylvania Fireside Tales Volume I*. For now, suffice it to say that a drive through Clark's Valley and onto its surrounding mountain peaks is still especially pleasant and colorful in autumn when the trees set the hills ablaze with the vibrant colors of fall. The natural surroundings and beauty are apt to send thoughts back to the time of the Minskers when Indians, mountain lions, and wolves still made these same hills their home.

Then, too, if a closer sense of those times is desired, the reader may want to travel through here at night and savor the nocturnal surroundings. Stop and listen; if you listen closely enough, you may even be so fortunate

---

1. W. H. Egle, *History of the Counties of Dauphin and Lebanon in the Commonwealth of Pennsylvania*, 446–447.
2. Interviews with locals Jack Strawl (April 24, 1991) and Ralph Kinter (June 6, 1989).

to hear a sound from those olden times; the howl of a coyote from atop Third Mountain.

> **LOCATION:** **The King's Stool** can be found on Short Mountain above Clarks Valley in Dauphin County (DD GPS Coordinates: 40.3684202, -76.9616425). Along Route 322, take Route 225 North at the village of Dauphin. Follow 225 until an intersection with Route 325. Turn right to go east into Clark's Valley. Follow 325 about five miles. A path at a roadside farm on the right goes up the mountain to the King's Stool.

CHAPTER 2

STAIRWAYS TO THE STARS

There are intriguing places of mystery and wonder worldwide, and the United States, not surprisingly, has quite a few of its own. Such locales often become tourist attractions; many of these sites could be mentioned here. However, the Winchester Mystery House in San Jose, California, is a good starting point for our present chapter.

A private holding company now owns this sprawling Queen Anne Style Victorian mansion, but it was once the personal residence of Sarah Winchester, widow of William Winchester, founder of the Winchester Firearms Company. After he died in 1881, his wife, as his sole heir, became fabulously wealthy, but the fortune came with a price—a feeling of guilt about the many people killed by one of the firearms her husband had manufactured and sold.

Subsequently convinced by a medium that she should build a house to serve as a residence for the spirits of those victims, Mrs. Winchester commenced doing so. She was also convinced that as long as she kept adding to her mansion, no trouble would befall her or her family, so she continued building until her death in 1922.

Mrs. Winchester acted as architect, adding rooms and stories to the house in a haphazard way, with no master plan to guide her. The final result was a perplexing complex that needed to be constructed that way, she believed, to confuse and ward off malevolent spirits. Consequently, some windows only overlook the interiors of other rooms rather than provide an outside view of the land on which the mansion stands. There are also doors that, when opened, only expose a solid wall and, probably most curious, sets of stairs that lead to nowhere.[1] However, the tales of baffling staircases in the castles and manor houses of the British Isles seem to hold the greatest fascination for those who enjoy these types of stories, and there are plenty of those accounts to go around.

Architects who have studied the construction of the ancient stone stairways found in many of these medieval fortifications have noted one common feature; the stairs within were constructed so that random steps were of uneven height. These so-called "stumble steps" were included, it is thought, so that attackers running up the steps would stumble and fall, thus slowing them down.[2] But the accounts of ghosts haunting these same flights of stairs deter intruders today.

One of the most notable examples is the staircase in Raynham Hall, Norfolk, England, where an image of the "Brown Lady" appears on a photo of the hall's staircase in 1936. The photo caused quite a stir in ghost-hunting circles and seemed to authenticate the authenticity of sightings of this same spirit that have been reported for over two-hundred and fifty years.[3]

Likewise, Berry Pomeroy Castle, near Devon, England, is said to be haunted by the ghost of Margaret de Pomeroy, whose spirit haunts this ancient citadel's 15th-century winding stone staircase that leads down to the dungeon where she was imprisoned and starved to death.[4]

Similarly, the "Black Lady," said to be the ghost of a nun that haunts the premises of Tamworth Hall in Staffordshire, England, is yet another spirit that glides noiselessly through that ancient castle's many winding stairways and dark corridors.[5]

But perhaps the most fantastic of all these stairways in the British Isles is the one near Beetham in Cumbria, England, that locals call the "Fairy Steps." Rectangular stone steps, so symmetrical that they were not randomly fashioned by forces of nature, lead up through a narrow crevice formed by two gigantic rock ledges. However, the steps are so small and the

---

1. Mary Jo Ignoffo, *Captive of the Labyrinth*, and at www.winchestermysteryhouse.com.
2. Sidney Toy, *Castles, Their Construction and History*, 91.
3. Richard Jones, *Haunted Britain and Ireland*, 80–81.
4. Ibid., 18.
5. Ibid., 102, and J. A. Brooks, *Britain's Haunted Heritage*, 93–94.

The Fairy Steps, Cumbria, England. (Photo Courtesy of David Ross and Britain Express.)

corridor so narrow that humans find walking up or down the passageway impossible without touching its stone walls.

Hence the belief that the steps were placed there by fairies and that if you make a wish at the top of the stairs and manage to walk down and not touch the walls, the fairies will grant your wish.[6] This stairway serves as a nice segue into the mysterious stone stairways found in the mountains of Pennsylvania.

I've never found any stone stairways on Pennsylvania mountainsides that are said to be the product of elfin hands, nor have I discovered any that are thought to be haunted in some way, but there are impressive flights of stone steps on different Pennsylvania mountain slopes that may present the occasional hiker who comes upon them unexpectedly for the first time with as much of a mystery as the Fairy Steps do to hikers initially encountering those odd stone steps in England.

To these Pennsylvania hikers, the questions must naturally arise as to who built these "flights of fancy," that appear to be nothing more than that, and why they did so. However, a little research usually confirms why they

---

6. Jones, Ibid., 137–138.

A Section of the Thousand Steps on Jacks Mountain. (Photo courtesy of Rusty Glessner, Rusty Glessner Photography.)

are there and who built them, and several notable examples can be cited to illustrate this point.

Of course, one of the most well-known landmarks is the Thousand Steps in Huntingdon County, but Showers' Steps in Berks County, Fox's Path in Perry and Cumberland Counties, and the Indian Steps in Huntingdon County are other notable examples as well.

The Thousand Steps Trail is a section of the rugged Standing Stone Trail that passes through Jack's Narrows—a wild defile steeped in history and legendary lore and which passes between the local communities of Mount Union and Mapleton Depot.

The Trail takes its name from the many stone steps found here that extend up the mountainside, and, it is said, actually number one thousand and forty-three. Their presence in such a remote spot may seem quite mysterious, but a large historical marker here sheds some light on that mystery.

The sign explains that on the mountaintop at one time was a large quarry where the Harbison-Walker fire brick company employees quarried the vast deposits of ganister rock, or Tuscarora sandstone, found here. Initially, a dinky train was used to transport the rocks to the fire brick refractories below, and workers could ride them up to the quarries. However, when trucks began replacing the trains, workers climbed the steep mountain to get to their place of work. Then, during an idle work period in 1936, the company had their men build the steps up the mountain to make their daily climbs easier.

Those are the steps that remain here yet today, and the pathway is considered by many to be one of the most popular hiking trails in that area. And the rewards for those reaching the summit are some of the finest panoramic views in the state. Vistas of Jack's Narrows, glimpses of Huntingdon, Mapleton, and Mount Union, and cascading mountain ranges fading off in the distance make the climb worthwhile.

Similarly, according to local sources, the stone steps on the Blue Mountain above the small town of Bethel in Berks County were constructed for an identical purpose by the Showers brothers in the 1930s. Lloyd Showers and his brother thought having an easy access path to the Appalachian Trail on the mountaintop above would be nice, so they spent months laying out their stone stairway. Hikers still use the staircase today and refer to it as Showers' Steps. The stone steps provide a good aerobic workout for those who make the ascent to enjoy panoramic views of the Tulpehocken Valley.

Then there is a stone-bordered pathway on the Blue Mountains near a scenic mountain pass called Sterrett's Gap that connects the counties of Perry and Cumberland. Residents of the nearby villages of Dromgold and Sherman's Dale refer to it as Fox's Path, preserving the memory of the man who built it.

It is not a staircase, but a dirt path demarcated on both sides, its entire length by high stone walls that consist of loose boulders piled on top of one another. The pathway begins in Perry County near Fox's Hollow, a

The author on the Indian Steps, Tussey Mountain, Huntingdon County.

remote mountain glen named after the first settler here. He was a farmer or trapper who frequently traveled to Carlisle in Cumberland County and blazed this shortcut over the mountain. It was a rocky path, and to make it an easier trek, he threw the rocks on it to the sides until he had a smoother rock-free trip.[7]

So the provenance of many seemingly out-of-place stone stairways found in the Pennsylvania mountains can still be found if the right sources are consulted. However, one remarkable span of stone steps on Tussey Mountain in Huntingdon County has mysterious origins. The Indian Steps, as they are called, seem to belie their origin in the name assigned

---
7. Information obtained through interviews with local hiking enthusiasts in 1980 and 2001.

Another view of the Indian Steps. Leading up from Harrys Valley Road on the south side of Tussey Mountain, Huntingdon County, and ending on the Mid State Trail on the mountaintop.

to them. Many early folklorists promoted the idea that Indians built this staircase for military purposes. However, any research into how Indians waged war will easily prove this theory to be nothing more than a myth, a good story that adds to the romance of the mountains.

In the first place, meticulous historian Paul A. W. Wallace, in his *Indian Paths of Pennsylvania,* makes no mention of any such Indian path over Tussey Mountain and down to Rock Springs. Furthermore, the Indian origins of the steps were not supported by the gentlemen I like to call, who said he would not object to my doing so, "the grandfather of the Mid State Trail." In my conversations with Tom Thwaite, planner and developer of

The stone cairn along the Mid State Trail. Marking the intersection of the Mid State Trail with the end of the Indian Steps Trail on top of Tussey Mountain, Huntingdon County, the cairn frowns down upon the village of Rock Spring, Centre County, at the base of the mountain and to the north.

that highly popular hiking trail across the state, I asked him about the famous steps and who built them.

He agreed that it was not Native Americans and postulated that the best explanation for their existence was that the landholder of that section of mountain timberland felt he needed to create a prominent boundary line between his land and that of a local iron company's adjacent lands. Driven by a fear that in their insatiable need for wood to fuel their iron furnaces, the iron masters would indiscriminately cut down his timber, he built the steps in what must have been a back-breaking and seemingly endless task.

We'll never know if that was how the steps came to be, but perhaps that means they will continue to provide the same sense of mystery and romance that have colored one of Pennsylvania's most impressive mountain landmarks over the years.

LOCATIONS:

Thousand Steps Trail is in Huntingdon County (DD GPS Coordinates: 40.39169, -77.91420). From the small town of Mount Union in Huntingdon County, follow U. S. Route 22 for a little over two miles. Look for a gravel parking area on the right. The Thousand Steps trailhead is at the parking lot's south end.

Indian Steps Trail is in Huntingdon County (DD GPS Coordinates: 40.6608988, -77.9786145). From State College in Centre County, Follow Route 26 south to the village of Pine Grove Mills. At the traffic light, turn left to continue on Route 26. Continue on Route 26 to the top of Tussey Mountain. Near a sweeping turn at the bottom of the descent down the mountain, look for Harry's Valley Road to the right. Follow this dirt road for about two miles, looking for the Indian Steps trail sign on the right.

Showers' Steps can be found in Berks County (DD GPS Coordinates: 40.471331448, -77.1730371). Follow Route 78 in Berks County to the Route 501 intersection near the town of Bethel. Follow Route 501 (Lancaster Avenue) north for two to three miles. Trailhead is on the right.

Fox's Path is in Perry County (DD GPS Coordinates: 40.3242526, -77.1730371). Along Route 11-15 in Perry County, take Valley Street onto Route 850 (Valley Road) near Marysville. Continue to travel west toward Sherman's Dale. Turn left onto Route 34 South (Spring Road) at the Sherman's Dale Post Office. Fox Hollow Road will be on the right after traveling one to two miles.

CHAPTER 3

UMBRELLA ROCK

When first trying to decide if there are enough unusual mountain landmarks in Pennsylvania to fill a book about them, I came across references to Umbrella Rock in Elk County. When I discovered pictures of this site, I was dumbfounded and convinced that if I ever wrote a book about Pennsylvania's mountain landmarks, Umbrella Rock should be one of the highlights. And like the other places I wanted to include in the book, I wanted to go there personally and take pictures. That task, however, proved to be as difficult as it was for many of the other rock formations I had identified and wanted to visit in person.

Many of these places are not easily accessible or found, which may be a blessing in disguise. The fact that they are inaccessible and somewhat hidden away protects them from the vandalism I had previously discovered in at least one sad case (more on this in a chapter to be included in Volume 2). But it also made my task to find Umbrella Rock quite frustrating.

Despite my initial attempts to find it on two separate occasions, the rock remained aloof, and in my exploratory treks, it had taxed my physical limits and patience. Therefore, I decided I needed a local guide to help me find it. Fortunately, I found such a man, a kindred spirit who is as driven to preserve local history and lore as much as I am.

Local guide Bob Ingham knows the Elk County Mountains around Ridgway better than any man and, in his friendly and engaging way, conducted me to a gated forestry road that winds its way up a local mountain that was once called Chestnut Ridge, owing to the profusion of American

Umbrella Rock, as seen from below.

The author at Umbrella Rock, giving perspective as to size.

chestnut trees that once grew on its slopes. Today the chestnut trees are gone, wiped out by the chestnut blight, but at over 2,000 feet in height; the ridge can still claim the honor of being one of the highest points in that region. However, it's most well-known for the fantastic eroded sandstone sculptures that can be found on its peak, and it was those formations that I came here to find.

As we got closer to the curious formation that drew me to this spot in the first place, my guide regaled me with historical details about the area and kept branching off the main path to show me other interesting rock formations along the way, including one that looked like petrified logs crowned it, and others that were precariously balanced stacks of boulders. There were also numerous rock overhangs, many of which he thought could have been used as rock shelters by the local Indians that once frequently traveled through here on their numerous paths that crisscrossed the ridge.

In talking about the shelters, he also mentioned the Split Rock Shelter, located about six miles from Umbrella Rock on this same ridge. Archeologists have made numerous excavations and concluded that Native Americans used it over 6,000 years ago.[1] But it was a rock shelter containing artifacts of more recent vintage that my guide wanted me to see and which was along the path ahead. This one, which archeologists have designated the Pinnacle Rock shelter (Pinnacle Rock being another name locals use to refer to Umbrella Rock), owing to its proximity to Umbrella Rock, became famous not only for the artifacts found there but also as a burial site.

The archeologists were drawn here when human remains were discovered in the deep cavity. The flexed skeleton was remarkably well preserved and determined to be that of a Native American woman of about 42. Since no other burials were found nearby, it was thought that she may have died while traveling through the area. If so, it's remarkable how carefully she was laid to rest.

Her traveling companions must have respected her highly since she had been buried with many artifacts, including a box turtle shell that formed a sort of pillow for her head, a sharpened bone awl, mussel shells, and an ornate, nearly intact ceramic vessel, which had been placed in her hands.[2]

---

1. James T. Herbstritt and David A. Love, "Archeological Investigations of Split Rock Shelter" *Pennsylvania Archeologist*, Vo. 45, No. 4, 1975.
2. Lee Burkett, "A Rockshelter Burial in Northwestern Pennsylvania," *Pa. Archeologist*, Vol. 47, 1977, p. 48.

Pinnacle Rock Shelter. The remains of the Indian woman found buried here were transferred to the Carnegie Museum of Natural History in Pittsburgh. There she lies, resting peacefully today (but not under starry skies).

Inspection and analysis of the design on the vessel led some scholars to believe that it could date back as far as the early fourteenth century, which would make it over 700 years old. Not nearly as ancient as the 6,000-year-old artifacts found at the Split Rock Shelter or the Meadowcroft Rockshelter located in Jefferson Township of Washington County. Archeologists believe it was a site of human habitation for over 19,000 years. If dated accurately, it would make it the earliest known evidence of human presence, if not the longest sequence of continuous human occupation, in the New World.[3]

Although seven-hundred years would seem like a mere blip compared to 19,000 years, it is enough time to have erased the story associated with the Indian woman so carefully laid to rest near Umbrella Rock. But even though her life story is forever lost to us, she lives on in the archeological record of her burial place.

There, in a rock shelter surrounded by a forest of hemlock, mountain laurel, and vestiges of old apple orchards, the last remnants of the

---

3. Nikhil Swaminathan, "Meadowcroft Rock Shelter," *Archaeology*, Sept./Oct. 2014.

The "logs" – "stacked" on the left side of the rocks, near Umbrella Rock, Elk County.

More rocky towers near Umbrella Rock, Elk County.

settlements of those employed by the lumbering industry once so prominent here, her former resting place remains. And on the forest floor, dense areas of wild blackberry, burdock, sweet fern, buck thorn, and Devil's Club thrive while thick vines of wild grape ensnarl the surrounding rocks and trees. It would look familiar to those who laid her to rest in this hallowed spot, as would nearby Umbrella Rock, where those same tribesmen may have huddled for shelter against the cold winds of winter from time to time and which they may have even regarded with superstitious awe because of its seemingly impossible balancing act.

LOCATION: Umbrella Rock is in State Game Lands #44 near Ridgway, Elk County (DD GPS Coordinates: 41.3367281, -78.8166969). Take Route 219 South out of Ridgway to Snowdrift Road on the right. Turn right onto Snowdrift Road and then into a Game Commission Parking Lot. There is a gated Game Commission Road right next to the parking area. Go through the gate and turn left onto the road that is the old Shawmut & Ridgway Railroad grade. Follow the grade until it is blocked, then bear to the right to continue on the Game Commission road. Follow the road until you see a small rock formation on your right. Proceed down the hill about 100 yards; on your left is a trail leading back to the Umbrella Rock formation.

CHAPTER 4

THE THREE SISTERS

Although it might be included among the rockiest hikes that anyone can take in Pennsylvania, the section of the Standing Stone Trail that passes through Rocky Ridge Natural Area in Huntingdon County is also the most awe-inspiring and, in the springtime, one of the most beautiful. From late spring into early summer, numerous wildflowers turn the mountain here into a vibrant palette of colorful hues, including delicate lady slippers of pink and white, putty-root orchids with their small yellow blossoms, and the rare Virginia Pennywort (*obolaria Virginica*), which only grows here and in one other place in Pennsylvania, with its purple and white flowers.[1]

However, the immense sandstone and limestone boulders that line the mountaintop make this a special place. Standing upright like silent sentinels guarding the secrets that might be hidden here, the massive rocks create labyrinthine passageways that demand a hiker's undivided attention. But there are appealing distractions nearby, including the Thousand Steps Trail (see the "Stairways to the Stars" chapter for details) and Jack's Narrows, deemed the deepest water gap in the state.[2] It has a dark history.

It can be said that of all the secrets that the standing stones on Rocky Ridge are guarding, one of the foremost would be the location of the gravesite of Jack Armstrong, an early Indian trader who is said to have been murdered by Indians about a mile due east of the Thousand Steps Trail

---
1. Information found on the Standing Stone Trail webpage at www.standingstonetrail.org.
2. "Jacks Narrows Pa," found on the web at www.raystown.org.

The author amongst the rocks on Rocky Ridge

and near where two major American Indian paths, the Frankstown Path and the Juniata Path, once converged. Jack's Mountain and Jack's Narrows are thought to be named for him, and ghostly lights on Rocky Ridge were once thought to have revealed his resting place (a story about the "Standing Stone" will appear in *Volume 2*).

This area is also home to impressive stone displays that stir the imagination. Here can be found Hunter's Rocks, a favorite destination for climbers who consider it one of the best sections for bouldering in Pennsylvania and perhaps on the entire east coast.[3] Then, too, there are several stacks of rocks that, in their impossible piling, seem to defy gravity itself (more details and pictures about these "Ho-doo" rocks will also appear in *Volume 2*).

---

3. "Hunters," found on the web at www.rockclimbing.com.

Sailboat Rock.

Here too, are rocks of such varied shapes and surface features that they seem to be imported from another world entirely. One such fantastic monolith is a large upright single wedge resting on a larger base, which, when I first saw it, reminded me of a sailboat. Hence, I could not resist naming it Sailboat Rock, even though someone else may have already assigned a different name.

Along this same trail, I also passed by a rock that, when viewed from a certain angle, struck me as some sort of ritual object that might have come right from the Aztec jungles of South America or maybe even from the Indiana Jones *Temple of Doom* movie set. At least, this was my thought when I saw a face looking back at me when I first looked at the rock.

However, this was not a new experience since I often see faces in the rocks when hiking in these rocky places. That might seem a cause for concern, but psychologists have a name for it. Pareidolia, they say, is a common psychological phenomenon that causes the human brain to lend significance—and facial features, in particular—to random patterns.

Sailboat Rock from a different angle.

The face in the rocks. A grotesque visage, hiding between the two trees on the right and guarding the Standing Stone Trail.

A view of Oregon's Three Sisters.

But then, a final surprise awaits the adventurer who chooses to explore this unique spot. At some point along the trail, the hiker comes to a sign indicating they are entering the "Three Sisters Natural Area." No signs here give any details as to the origin of that name, and Internet searches shed no further light on it either. But there are other like-named areas throughout the world, with two of the most notable being in this country and a third, more famous one located in Australia,

In the U. S. state of Oregon, the Three Sisters are three closely spaced volcanic peaks among the highest in that state,[4] while in the Potomac River near Washington D. C., there are three rocky islands also known as the Three Sisters. In the case of the Oregon peaks, there appears to be no information as to why that name was assigned to them, but why the Potomac islands have that name is revealed in a Native American legend that has survived to this day.

According to the legend, the islands are said to have been named for three Algonquian Indian sisters who rejected the husbands their father had picked out for them and who, as punishment, marooned them on the islands in the deepest part of the river. The three women supposedly cursed this spot by proclaiming that if they could not escape across the river here, no one would ever be able to do so. Since then, legend holds that when someone attempting to cross the river here is about to fall victim to the

---

4. "Geology and History Summary for Three Sisters," and public domain photo found on the web at www.USGS.gov/volcanoes/three-sisters.

A view of Austrailia's Three Sisters.

curse, the waters seem to emit a moaning or bell-like sound as though announcing its intention of claiming its next victim.[5]

Worldwide, however, the most famous area, the Three Sisters, is an unusual rock formation in Australia's Blue Mountains. It is one of that country's most popular tourist attractions, and it takes its name from an Aboriginal legend about three sisters who were turned to stone. The relative position of the Australian rocks to one another and the ancient legend told about them are strikingly similar to the legend and relative positions of the three rocks known as the Three Sisters on Rocky Ridge and perhaps provide a clue as to why the Pennsylvania rocks have the same name.

According to what is identified as an Australian aborigine "dream-time" legend, the three sisters, whose names are recalled as Meehni, Wilah, and Gunnedoo, were once courted by three brothers from another tribe. Since tribal law forbade them to marry, the tribes went to war when the brothers planned to kidnap their sweethearts. During the conflict, the sisters were

---

5. Charles Skinner, *Myths and Legends of Our Own Land*, 218.

The Three Sisters on Rocky Ridge, Rocky Ridge Natural Area, Huntingdon County, Pennsylvania.

turned to stone by a tribal elder trying to protect them, but he was killed in the warfare, and no one knew how to change the sisters back into human form![6]

Although the legend of the Three Sisters rock formation on Pennsylvania's Rocky Ridge has not been preserved over time, it may have been rooted in the tales of our native peoples, just like the legend of Australia's Three Sisters. It seems entirely possible that someone familiar with our Native American culture thought it appropriate to use that designation for this rocky pile. At least it seemed like a good place to begin an investigation, and what better place to start than with the legendary lore of the Iroquois Nation in Pennsylvania.

They call themselves the *Haudenosaunee*, or "People of the Longhouse," and in their *Longhouse Legends*, the Three Sisters legend is recalled as part of the Iroquois creation myth, but it is also explained as to why the Iroquois consider three crops, corn, beans and squash, to be special gifts from the

---

6. Found on the Blue Mountains Australia website at www.bluemts.com.au.

Creator. These "sustainers of life," so considered among Native Americans, are always planted together, a traditional gardening technique for untold generations.[7]

The practice was found to be effective, which has been confirmed by modern-day horticulturalists, who have noted the synergistic benefits. The tall corn stalks provide sturdy support for the vining beans, which return nitrogen to the soil, a beneficial enhancement that spurs other plants' growth. And not to be outdone, the large leaves of the squash plants shade the soil and trap the moisture the growing crops need. From this apparent beneficial interdependence, the Iroquois sagely concluded that the three crops should always be planted together and that each of the three crops is protected by one of the Three Sister Spirits.[8]

From this belief came numerous Native American legends about those spirits and how they never wanted to be parted from one another. The account recorded by the Oneida Indian Nation in New York State begins, as many of the Longhouse stories begin, with "Long time ago . . . ," and recalls that there was once a family of a mother, a father and their three daughters; three sisters who drove their parents to distraction.

It seems that it was all the parents could do to provide the necessities for their family, but rather than being able to rely on their daughters for assistance, they had to beg them for it and to intercede in their constant quarrels.

Apparently, their clashing personalities caused such friction between the children. Each one was as different from the other as siblings can be in physical appearance and personality. The oldest sister was said to be tall and slender with long silky hair that shone like gold in the sunlight; the youngest sister was smaller in stature and considered attractive even though more muscular. The middle sister was of average height and looks but was beautiful in her giving nature.

Although their sisterly love bound them, they still could not resist arguing over the smallest slight or lack of cooperation. Their bickering often interfered with the tasks they were supposed to do, resulting in

---

7. Jesse Cornplanter, *Legends of the Longhouse*.
8. "The Three Sisters: Sustainers of Life," found at the Carnegie Museum of Natural History website https://nsew.carnegiemnh.org/Iroquois-confederacy-of-the-northeast/three-sisters.

it falling upon the parents to do them instead. Then one year, when it was planting time, and the gardening was not getting done; the parents became concerned that they would not survive the winter without provisions in store.

Nothing they did could dissuade their daughters from arguing and turning to the important tasks at hand. In desperation, the mother and father prayed to their harvest gods to do anything to help. Then as the parents watched their daughters argue loudly in the fields, they were amazed to see them transformed into three plants they'd never seen before. The first was a long, tall plant with silky tassels that looked like hair, the second was a low-growing plant with broad green leaves, and the third was of medium-height with long, tender vines.

This was the origin, so concludes the Oneida legend, of corn, squash, and beans, which they thereafter referred to as "The Three Sisters."[9] The tale became so widely disseminated that whenever Native Americans saw three large upright rocks nearby, they must have been reminded of the legend, thus prompting them to assign that title to the rocks. Certainly speculation on my part, but probably as good an explanation as any that can be offered today.

> **LOCATION:** The Standing Stone Trail can be found in the Rocky Ridge Natural Area of Rothrock State Forest near Martin's Gap of Huntingdon County (DD GPS Coordinates: 40.3390, -77.5093). From State College, take Route 26 south to the village of McAlevey's Fort. About a mile from town, you will come to a stop sign and turn left to stay on Route 26. Continue on Route 26 for about five miles until you see Martin's Gap road on the left. Turn left onto Martin's Gap Road and continue about a mile until you see a bridge on the left. Cross the bridge and make an immediate right. Drive on this road for approximately one mile, and at a Y intersection, bear right onto Frew Road. Here is a parking area for the trailhead leading onto the Standing Stone Trail and into Rocky Ridge Natural Area.

---

9. "The Legend of the Three Sisters," found on the Oneida Nation website at www.oneidaindiannation.com/the-legend-of-the-three-sisters.

CHAPTER 5

LEWIS' ROCK

On a dark and uninviting summit atop the South Mountain of Michaux State Forest, Cumberland County, a collection of towering rock walls is among the most celebrated of all those in the Pennsylvania highlands. The imposing rock ramparts form a confusing maze of passages and tunnels that could serve as a refuge for men and animals alike. As noted in other chapters in this volume, Pennsylvania's rock cities have provided shelter for wild animals large and small, and, with so many deep crevices and small caverns, no doubt continue to do so. Thus, it may surprise some that the rock city on Michaux State Forest's South Mountain once served as a shelter for one of Pennsylvania's most notorious outlaws. And so, the term "shelter" for this spot is misleading, with the words "hideout" or "robber's den" being more historically accurate.

In future volumes, we also will describe two other unique mountain landmarks in Michaux State Forest: Rothrock's Rock, named after Pennsylvania's first state forester, and Sentinel Rock, named by local Indians in memory of a warrior who failed as a nocturnal sentry assigned to warn his tribe of approaching enemy warriors. On the other hand, Lewis Rocks is named for the infamous Davy Lewis, who favored this spot as a hideaway when trying to evade the many lawmen trying to arrest him.

The story of Davy Lewis, popularly known at one time as "Robber Lewis" and, paradoxically by some as "the Robin Hood of Pennsylvania," has become so suffused with legend and romance over the years that it is hard today to know exactly how much is fact and how much is fancy. But historians generally agree that David Lewis was born in Carlisle, Pennsylvania, sometime in 1790. Shortly afterward, his family settled along the banks of Bald Eagle Creek at the famous "Eagle's Nest," the former site of Indian chief Bald Eagle's village at present-day Milesburg.[1]

David's father, Lewis, and Lewis's wife, Jane, had moved here after the father, an accomplished surveyor, had been appointed by the Provincial Government of Pennsylvania to survey the area in and around what is now Centre County. His surveying work included laying out the town of Lewistown, present-day Mifflin County, and some claim that the town was named after him.

Within a year of settling at "the Eagle's Nest," Lewis was badly injured by a falling tree while surveying land along the Juniata River, dying shortly thereafter in a hospital at Lewistown. His death left his widow Jane with eight children, ranging in age from her infant David to the oldest at eighteen.

The determined Jane, falling back on an independent and determined spirit inherited from her Irish ancestors, struggled to keep her family together and provide for them. But she could not handle all the chores on her own, so she took on an Indian woman with a young girl named Cynthia, whom many thought was the Indian woman's daughter. Jane and her two hired women kept things going until, a year after her first husband's death; she married her neighbor, widower Frederick Leathers.

Together they ran Frederick's farming, lumbering, and distillery businesses, but then the family's fortunes declined again when, in 1796, Frederick died, leaving Jane a widow a second time. Once again, faced with a family to take care of and running the farm and businesses she had inherited, she turned to her children to help pull the load. Even young Davy, only six years old, pitched in to do family chores and work odd jobs to supplement the family income.[2]

As a hired farm hand over the years, he would help "grub" fields to clear out roots and stumps, haul dung from stables, and roll logs down mountain slopes to be carted off to sawmills. The work no doubt toughened him physically, but perhaps during this time, he developed the "devil-may-care"

---

1. James P. Burke, *Pioneers of Second Fork*, 50-52, and Mac E. Barrick, "Who was Lewis the Robber?" *Cumberland County History*, 55, and C. D. Rishel, *Life and Adventures of Lewis*, 34–35.
2. Rishel, Ibid., 34–35.

fearless attitude that seemed to be one of his distinguishing characteristics later in life. It was a trait he would have needed to develop when, as a six-year-old, he often had to walk back home accompanied by the cries of mountain lions and howls of wolves echoing through a darkening forest at the end of his workday.

But despite their valiant efforts, the family could not make ends meet on the farm, so Jane took up general nursing and midwifery work to close the financial gap.

In 1802 she finally moved to the Clearfield County town of Clearfield, bringing her moonshine distillery and devoting herself to her midwifery. As a result of her dedicated and faithful service in that profession, she became highly respected and well-liked, with locals eventually affectionately referring to her as "Granny Leathers."

Probably highly pleased and content with the fruits of her labor, Jane Lewis had no idea of the disappointments that her son Davy would someday lay at her doorstep. Davy continued to help his mother until, at age 17, he decided he needed to see the world and ran off to Bellefonte to join the army. His enlistment only lasted a year when he decided the army wasn't for him, so he deserted.

Several months later, he reenlisted under an assumed name but was shortly thereafter discovered to be a deserter and sentenced to death by firing squad. As a result of pleas from his mother and from the fact he was still a minor, his sentence was changed to a long jail sentence. But after only a short incarceration in the jail at the Carlisle Army Barracks, the intractable Lewis escaped after picking the lock on his ball and chain and leaving it on the floor of his jail cell. The ease with which he escaped would later become another skill for which he became infamous.[3]

Lewis was then a wanted man, and it marked the start of his crime spree, which no doubt appealed to his self-described "rambling disposition." [3] He pursued a life of crime, often robbing the rich to give to the poor. So much so, in fact, that it would eventually lead some to compare him to England's Robin Hood and Robert Roy MacGregor, the "Rob Roy" of Scottish fame—two altruistic outlaws of the British Isles.[4]

---

3. Rishel, Ibid., 37–39.
4. Rishel, Ibid., 7.

After escaping from the Carlisle barracks, Lewis made his way to a cave he knew about along the banks of Condoguinet Creek in Cumberland County above Newville. The damp uninviting cavern would serve as a refuge for him now and again in the future, along with similar caverns throughout the state, and eventually, this one became known as "Lewis's Cave."[5]

Another Cumberland County cavern was often frequented by Lewis and may have been his favorite. This one, also to become known as Lewis's or the Robber's Cave, was located in the Doubling Gap near the Perry/Cumberland County border. It may have been Lewis's favorite cavern because it proved to be an ideal hiding place, and as one of his associates who once shared it with him would later state, it was "so comfortably arranged in and about the cave that it was quite a comfortable home."[6]

But it also proved to be a safe haven since the outlaws had formed a friendship with a neighbor whose house they could see from the cave. The outlaws knew that the obliging neighbor, who sympathized with them, would fly a red flag from the house's front porch post when any lawmen were in the area. When the coast was clear, a white flag would be flown instead.

From their various underground hiding places, and it was believed that they "were familiar with every hiding-place in the state,"[7] the bold bandits engaged in a "reign of terror" robbing stage coaches and lone travelers, and it was thought that they hid those ill-gotten gains, thousands of dollars in gold and silver coins, in those same hiding places. But at some point, Lewis's sixth sense seemed to warn him that the law might be closing in, and then, after having a falling out with his associates, he silently snuck out of the cavern where they were hiding at the time.

From here, he rambled far and wide, from Vermont to Canada, spreading counterfeit bills and establishing himself at the top of the "most wanted" lists everywhere he went. He eventually went back to New York State, where he was caught passing bogus bills, and in Troy, he was put in jail, but he managed to escape again.

---

5. Rishel, Ibid., 19.
6. Rishel, Ibid., 69.
7. Rishel, Ibid., 29.

Later described as an "Adonis" in physical stature,[8] he was also born with a "silver tongue," a combination the opposite sex found hard to resist. He used it to his advantage more than once, to the point where it was said he could "charm the pants off a preacher's wife," In Troy, he used it to entice the jailer's daughter to help him escape.[9]

He subsequently fell in with other miscreants of his ilk, who convinced him that he should return to Pennsylvania "where a great portion of the population were credulous, ignorant, unsuspicious, and easy to be imposed upon."[10] Thus, he began another round of robberies and counterfeiting from Philadelphia to Pittsburgh. Teamsters driving Conestoga wagons, people in private conveyances, and stagecoaches were stopped and held at gunpoint throughout Cumberland, Adams, York, Perry, Mifflin, Franklin, and Centre Counties, and the crimes seemed to go on with impunity, despite Lewis being caught and imprisoned twice; once in Bedford and another time in Chambersburg.

But true to form, the infamous thief managed to escape from those jail cells too easily, and time and time again, he eluded posse after posse looking for him, almost as though he could vanish into thin air, another quality which he seemed to possess as he evaded permanent capture for years. The narrow escapes seemed to fuel his ego and his need for adrenaline rushes, as he would later describe the pursuits as "fox hunts," where "the fox always got away." [8]

Many stories are told of Lewis's boldness and his success in evading capture, and after he escaped from the jail in Chambersburg, it is recalled that he made his way to Harrisburg, where he secluded himself behind some barrels and drygoods boxes in front of a general store on the east shore. Here he remained until the evening when it was customary for a group of regulars to gather around the store's pot-bellied stove to exchange stories and gossip.

Among the most widely discussed topics of the day were those of Lewis the Robber, and several of the self-important windbags began to brag about how they'd "cuff him around" and "cart him off to jail" should they ever

---

8. John B. Linn, op. cit., 62.
9. Burke, op. cit., 52.
10. Rishel, op. cit., 46.

encounter him. The whole time Lewis had to restrain himself until, unable to contain himself any longer, he rose to his full height, upsetting the pile of boxes he had been hiding behind. The crashing boxes made a terrible racket, but Lewis's stentorian voice could still be heard as he shouted, "I am Lewis the Robber. Take me if you dare!"

The effect was alarming, as all those in the store rushed to the nearest exits without regard to their surroundings. One man ran into a lamp post and severely skinned his nose; another thumped into stacked tar barrels, causing them to roll over. Another man, managing to get outside, raced across the street and stumbled into a pyramid of grind stones arranged at another store front. The crashing stones fell onto him, resulting in injuries so severe that he had to use crutches to get around for several weeks. The panicky retreats amused the bold outlaw, who calmly holstered his pistols and nonchalantly walked out the front door as though nothing had happened, leaving the deserted store in disarray.[11]

This insouciance would surface again close to his hideout in Lewis Rocks one day in present-day Cumberland County. A group of county men fed up with the impunity with which Lewis and his outlaws committed their crimes decided to form a posse to go after them. Somehow Lewis heard about the plan and decided to have fun at the men's expense. Learning about their location, he calmly rode up and expressed an interest in joining them. They gladly accepted his offer, figuring there was safety in numbers.

The search failed, and Davy shared his disappointment with the other men in the posse as they all went their separate ways. However, several days later, the Cumberland County sheriff got a letter that read, "I trust you did not find Lewis, the Robber, to be such a bad companion after all," signed Davy Lewis.[12]

Despite several incarcerations and attempts by posse after posse to reign him in, Lewis was never convicted of any crimes, despite the large rewards offered for his capture. But his luck finally ran out on June 30, 1820, when he and a criminal associate were surrounded by a posse along the Bennett Branch of the Sinnemahoning Creek near Driftwood.

---

11. "A Reminiscence of Sixty Years Ago: I am Lewis the Robber!—Take Me If You Dare." Article appearing July 9, 1877, in the Harrisburg Patriot newspaper of Harrisburg, Pa.
12. Rishel, op. cit., 24.

My late wife at some of the rocks at Lewis Rocks, Cumberland County.

After a brief exchange of gunfire, Lewis and his partner in crime, Connelly, were mortally wounded. Connelly died while being transported to the jail in Bellefonte, and Lewis died in that same jail a few weeks later.[13] But Lewis's exploits and fame did not die with him, particularly stories about the gold and silver coins he hid in his cavernous hiding places, which most people still believe to this day still await a discoverer.

Thus, treasure seekers still explore the Robber's Cave in Doubling Gap and Lewis's Cave along the banks of the Condoguinet near Newville. Many also wish they could investigate the passageways of the Indian Caverns, a former commercial cave no longer open to the public but where Lewis claimed he had buried some of his loot. Likewise, it is thought he had hidden some of his ill-gotten gains among the towering rocks at Lewis Rocks, a place now in private hands and also no longer open to the public.

Lewis Rocks is a cold sanctuary of dark shadows where silence reigns today but which, two-hundred years ago, may have echoed with the cries of horsemen looking for a desperado of fearsome import. It also may still

---

13. John B. Linn, op. cit., 61–63.

hold a treasure that that same desperado hid here but, to the best of anyone's knowledge, has never been found.

Footnote:

An interesting account related to Lewis's Cave in Doubling Gap describes a nearby stone cairn that could once be seen on the Blue Mountain near the headwaters of Doubling Gap Creek. This interesting mountain landmark is probably no longer there but was once reputed to mark the gravesite of an infamous Indian fighter of the Pennsylvania frontier known in folklore as "The Black Rifle" and "Captain Jack."[14]

Although he is now regarded as more of a folk hero rather than a real person, the exploits attributed to him are thought to be more of a composite of actual events in the lives of many well-known frontiersmen of that day. See the "Jack's Narrows" chapter in the author's *Pennsylvania Fireside Tales Volume 2* for more information on this interesting character.

> **LOCATION: Lewis' Rocks** is in Tumbling Run Game Preserve, a privately-owned hunting area in the middle of Michaux State Forest of Cumberland County and to the west of Pine Grove Furnace State Park. The Tumbling Run Hunting Club in Biglerville, Pa., should be contacted to get permission to enter the preserve (DD GPS Coordinates: 40.01370, -77.3661). From Gettysburg, head west on Route 30 for about 15 miles to Route 233 (Pine Grove Road). Stay on Route 233 North for 5 to 10 miles, then pull into a well-marked gravel turnoff on the left. Follow the trail and Tumbling Run into Tumbling Run Game Preserve. Keep the stream on your left as you ascend the mountain until the trail ends at Lewis Falls. On the right of the falls, take the climber's path to the top of the ridgeline and Lewis Rocks.

---

14. Rishel, op. cit., 17.

CHAPTER 6

INFERNAL EVIDENCE

Even though the original forests and their imposing forest giants are gone, some places in Pennsylvania still retain the Devil's trademark, stamped upon them by those who begrudged their presence. As a result, they are imbued with an air of mystery, and their imposing landscapes present a menacing aspect, qualities that appeal to any lover of the odd and mysterious. Since I include myself as one of those people, I was drawn to the places bearing the devil's name and took photos of each one.

These places were considered unnatural and inhospitable to humans, for the reasons that will be explained in a future *Volume 3* chapter titled "Satan's Handiwork," that early settlers felt they deserved to have derogatory names, and so tacked the devil's name onto each. But out of all of them, it seems that the Devil's Den stands out above the others as a place deserving of that association.

Of all the places where anyone might sense the presence of an evil entity, it would have to be on the blood-stained ground of a battlefield—much like that at Gettysburg. The sulfurous smells of gunpowder discharges, the thick smoke that envelopes a field of battle because of those discharges, the loud reports of that cannon and musket fire, the flashes and sparkles of those same explosions, and the cries and groans of dying men, all combine to make the sights and sounds of a battle in progress a hellish experience.

Union General William Tecumseh Sherman, leader of the famous March through Georgia in 1864, summed it up nicely when addressing the graduating class of Michigan Military Academy in 1879, "I am tired

The Devil's Dining Room at Bilger's Rocks, located in Clearfield County. See the chapter titled "Bilger's Rocks" for more details about, and photos of, this unique rock city.

and sick of war. Its glory is all moonshine. It is only those who have neither fired a shot nor heard the shrieks and groans of the wounded who cry aloud for blood, more vengeance, more desolation. War is hell."[1]

So Devil's Den at Gettysburg would certainly seem to warrant its name given the hellish clashes that occurred there from July 1st through 3rd in 1863, but as the following photos and anecdotes will show, other places were just as despised or were regarded with as much disdain as that notorious spot. And their names might be termed "infernal evidence" of that fact. A supposition that is strengthened when these places become even more somber as the last rays of gold and saffron sunlight fade away and darkness envelopes them.

It would not be surprising if Civil War vets would recall their war experiences as having been as close as anyone can get to experiencing what it must be like in hell without actually going there. And one such man could certainly have been Henry Harrison Bingham, who served with the 140th

---

1. John Bartlett, Familiar Quotations, 613b.

Pennsylvania at Gettysburg and was later awarded the Congressional Medal of Honor for his heroism at the Battle of the Wilderness in May of 1864.

In a letter written to his sister in Williamsport, Pa., dated July 18, 1863 (so the events, being just two weeks old, would still have been fresh in his mind), he described his experiences while defending Cemetery Ridge against Pickett's Charge on July 3rd, 1863:

> Dear Sister,
>
> Do not think I have forgotten you.
>
> I came safe and sound out of the last engagement, and have no objections to go into another tomorrow, provided that we whip them. Gettysburg was a hard-fought and fairly won battle. By the by, I will tell you how I spent my 4th of July night.
>
> About 8 o'clock in the evening, I laid myself on the ground (and it was wet and foggy at the time) to rest for the night. I had nothing to put under or above me (on the field, we take nothing in the shape of bed clothing).
>
> About 12 o'clock, I woke and found that I was in a complete pool of water that nearly covered me, and it was raining terribly. I got up and stood by, or rather against a tree until daylight, but unfortunately, this tree was within 20 or 30 feet of some hundred wounded, dying or dead Rebel soldiers, and together with the groans and cries for water and the rain, I passed the night, the remembrance of which I can never forget.
>
> I would not have been surprised to have found my hair gray; my agony at times was so intense. But that is only one of the side scenes in the great conflict. The morning after the battle, I went over all the battleground, and I saw that which gave rise to the old expression 'dead heaped upon dead!'[2]

There is yet another "hellish" place in a gap in Bald Eagle Mountain along Route 15 between White Deer and South Williamsport. This boulder field, covering two to three acres, has caught the eye of passersby since

---

2. George D. Wolfe, "July 4, 1863, Gettysburg, 'He Was There'," appeared in the Journal of the Lycoming County Historical Society, Volume 1, No. 4, October 1956, Williamsport, Pa.

The Devil's Dungeon at Bilger's Rocks, along a tight passageway between the Devil's Dining Room and the Devil's Kitchen, it resembles dungeons found in medieval castles in Europe.

early coaching days when stagecoach passengers, riding the stage between Northumberland and Williamsport, Lycoming County, looked upon the stones and wondered how they got there.

The number and strange purplish color of the boulders suggested that they were not of natural origin, and, not knowing about glaciation and how huge glaciers moved and deposited rocks back in the glacial age, the pundits of stagecoach days decided that the devil was responsible for putting them here.

He was carrying some turnips in his apron when he tripped, and the turnips tumbled out. Despite his best efforts, his satanic majesty could not

The Devil's Kitchen at Bilger's Rocks. Yet another devilish place at Bilger's Rocks, this rock city seems to have more than its share of places named after the lord of the underworld, who might feel right at home in this remote place of many interlocking and confusing passageways. It was because of this maze that I was grateful for the park guide who escorted me through it, and who pointed out the unique spots therein.

get them all gathered back up, and those that remained eventually became petrified, retaining their purplish color. This colorful tale gained credence when people who explored the odd garden of rocks told of hearing strange noises coming from far beneath them.

Perhaps some of them also knew about and told of sounds heard beneath a similar field of rocks in Clarks Valley of Dauphin County which locals dubbed "the Devil's Racecourse" because they thought the noise was akin to the noise that the devil's hooves would make as he raced around his racetrack in his underworld home.

The Devil's Den, located in Elk State Forest near Ridgway, Elk County. This uninviting spot is thought to have been named by local Civil War veterans, who, upon seeing it, were reminded of the infamous Devil's Den on the battlefield at Gettysburg. Not an unlikely prospect considering what they had been through.

The Devil's Den – a close-up view. The burnt-orange cast on the rocks, reminiscent of the descriptions of the reflections cast by the eternal fires of hell, may have been an added incentive for Civil War veterans to name this Elk County landmark after the master of that place of eternal damnation.

The Devil's Den at Gettysburg – stereographic view. Probably a staged shot set up by the Weavers of Hanover, Pa., who took many pictures of the Gettysburg battlefield to sell as stereographic views. The soldiers, positioned as "dead" and alive, are most likely veterans who had returned for the dedication of the Soldiers National Cemetery in November of 1863. Photo courtesy Pennsylvania Historical and Museum Commission, Archives and Manuscripts (MG 218 photo collection).

Devil's Den, 1996. Compare this view of Devil's Den with the 1863 view. This picture shows the same scene over 130 years later. Much has remained the same, but the Boy Scouts that were here this day livened up the scene considerably compared to the proceedings in 1863!

Even when geologists later explained that the odd pinkish/purplish color of the sandstone rocks in the Devil's Turnip Patch is due to their high concentration of iron oxide, the original name for this strange rock garden was not cast aside. It had become too much a part of the popular culture and lore of the area, and to this day, it remains the "Devil's Turnip Patch."[3]

But hope springs eternal, as the saying goes, and neither Satan nor his tricks could forestall the determined advance of frontier settlements. Every fresh spring morning and every beautiful sunset must have reminded those frontiersmen that a higher power was behind them and would help them overcome all, even the seemingly insurmountable stone barriers that dotted the landscape, many of which remain with us to this day. As are the names those early settlers gave to some of them, not to honor Satan but presumably to show how they refused to be intimidated by him.

Sunrise over the Bald Eagles.

---

3. "The Devil's Turnip Patch," appeared in The Philadelphia Record, December 1900. See also History of Lycoming County, Pa., 420.

The Devil's Den at Gettysburg as seen from Little Round Top.

The Devil's Turnip Patch.

The Devil's Chimney, another "devilish" spot, located in Mosquito Valley, Lycoming County. The Devil's Elbow Natural Area is also nearby! There was no smoke coming out of the twelve foot high stand-alone "chimney", at least on this day!

Footnote:

Other Pennsylvania landmarks and places have acquired the same dark-side appellation as those mentioned in this chapter. However, none have distinctive physical characteristics like those that are included herein. Nonetheless, one such place in Schuylkill County deserves mention here. Its story has been preserved by oral history alone, but it is a humorous tale that appears to preserve a picture of life in the earliest decade of the nineteenth century.

Ella Zerbey Elliott recalls the incident in her delightful *Blue Book of Schuylkill County* (published 1916), where she relates the account of "How Devil's Hole Was Named." Devil's Hole, or *Tuyful's Loch* in the Pennsylvania Dutch vernacular, is located along the Blue Mountains between Port

The Devils Racecourse, Clarks Valley, Dauphin County.

Clinton and Tamaqua. In author Elliott's opinion, the region is "among the wildest and most picturesque to be found anywhere, either in the United States or abroad."

It deserves that description, she suggests, because this wilderness is in a bowl-like depression interlaced with numerous short valleys. The valleys, separated by mountains on all sides, are, even on the sunniest days, darkened by the shadows of the towering peaks. This undulating topography and its shadowy half-light can make it easy for someone unfamiliar with the terrain to become confused and get lost, as one peddler from Orwigsburg is said to have found out one day in 1811.

According to the story, author Elliott relates the peddler as a familiar sight to those living along the Blue Mountains in the southern part of that country. He was often seen with his peddler's pack making his way along his normal route through the hills, but one day he did not return home at his usual time.

His family was alarmed, but the peddler finally returned three days later, looking "rather the worse for the experience." Upon being questioned, he had to admit that he had gotten turned around, and as darkness fell, he got lost in the tangled landscape. Being tired and exasperated, he explained it this way; "*Ich wahr drei tag im Tuyful's sie Loch, uhn bin yusht raus cumma*" ("I was three days in the Devil's Hole and am just now out").

"And," so says author Elliott, "Devil's Hole it has been called ever since!"[4]

Footnote 2:

There is another iconic formation associated with the devil in the Lehigh Gap between Carbon and Lehigh Counties near Schnecksville, Lehigh County. Looking exactly like a pulpit placed upon a rock ledge, it is so precariously placed that locals thought that only the devil could have put it there, and then only because he wanted a place to preach to the human race. Locals called it the "Devil's Pulpit", and it was a popular hiking destination for years. But some time ago the trail leading up to it was permanently closed following the death of a hiker who got too close to the precipitous cliff face, slipped, and tumbled onto the rocks below. I guess it's a devilish place after all! Consequently, no good quality photos of it could be found for this book, and, for all I know, it may no longer even be there!

LOCATIONS:

Bilger's Rocks: Can be found in a park of the same name in Clearfield County near the town of Grampian in Bloom Township (DD GPS Coordinates: 40.9939479, -78.5922485). From Clearfield, the County Seat of Clearfield County, follow Route 322 west and take the Route 219 exit. Follow Route 219 south. After passing Coffee Road on the left, look for Bilger's Rocks Road on the left. Follow this road for several miles until you see the parking area and the park on the left.

Devil's Den (Gettysburg): This iconic site can be found in Gettysburg National Military Park in Gettysburg (DD GPS Coordinates: 39.789819, -77.2394293). Route 30 takes you to Gettysburg, where a battlefield map can be purchased. Devil's Den is located in the middle of the battlefield near the intersection of Crawford and Warren Avenues below Little Round Top.

---

4. Ella Zerbey Elliott, Blue Book of Schuylkill County, 451.

Devil's Den (Elk County): Is located in State Game Lands #44 near Elk State Forest in Elk County (DD GPS Coordinates: 41.390339, -78.7303055). This amazing rock city is northwest of Umbrella Rock. Follow the trail at Umbrella Rock to make a steep climb up the mountain to Devil's Den.

Devil's Turnip Patch: This purplish rock field is seen on Bald Eagle Mountain along Route 15 between South Williamsport and the village of White Deer, Lycoming County (DD GPS Coordinates: 41.2167466, -76.9296871). Follow Route 15 south out of South Williamsport. Look for a fenced maintenance yard with long blue buildings and a small blue water tank on the right. The turnip patch is right beside it.

Devil's Chimney: Stands on the mountainside along Mosquito Valley Road south of the village of Duboistown, Lycoming County. Mosquito Creek flows along the mountain's base (DD GPS Coordinates: 41.225781, -77.0369123). Drive south on Valley Street / Jacks Hollow Road out of Duboistown. Look for Mosquito Valley Road and turn left onto it. Look for the concrete wall remnants of a dam in the creek to the left. Pull over into the parking area here. Walk back towards Duboistown about 50 to 100 yards. The chimney will be across the creek and on the mountainside above you.

CHAPTER 7

MEMENTO MORI

The term *Memento mori,* according to the Oxford English Dictionary, is a Latin term meaning 'remember that you [have to] die.' It was a term that took root during the growth of Christianity, and early Puritans, no strangers to death and fearful of what might lay beyond, embraced the idea wholeheartedly. Consequently, their tombstones are decorated with reminders that, inevitably, we all must face death.

The sometimes-nightmarish statues on their gravesites, or the skulls, skeletons, and demons that appear on their headstones, and in many medieval graveyards in Europe, may strike us as ghoulish today, but they were intended as reminders, or *Memento mori,* to the living. However, statues, crypts, and headstones with unusual epitaphs can still be found in old Pennsylvania graveyards that serve the same purpose.

But they also sometimes make us wonder what secrets lay buried with the earthly remains of those whose last resting place is demarcated by the grave markers which draw us to them. In my many explorations throughout the mountains and valleys of Pennsylvania, I've always enjoyed walking through old family cemeteries hidden amongst the trees along little-traveled byways, and I've often been surprised by what I've found.

The weathered grave monuments, with their moss and lichen-covered epitaphs, often show signs of neglect, as do the graveyards themselves. Long forgotten by descendants who seem to have no sentiments regarding their antecedents, the cemeteries become overgrown with weeds, their tombstones eventually becoming hidden by that same undergrowth and by the moldering compost of fallen leaves and decaying vegetation. Brown stalks of dead weeds and wildflowers shivering in the cold clasp of winter winds make these resting places even less inviting to those who want to pay last respects to their ancestors.

It doesn't take more than a few years of inattention until the old boneyards blend into the forest, their residents and stories erased by time. And as time continues to pass, the unchecked growth of aggressive species like staghorn sumacs, wood ferns, deadly nightshade, hawthorn and raspberry bushes, poison ivy, and stinging nettles can make these places more uninviting than they otherwise would be, even on the brightest days of the year.

When walking among the headstones of these secluded spots, it's hard not to think about the stories buried with those whose remains lie here. These repositories can be thought of as a library of sorts, a vault of rare manuscripts containing episodes from even centuries past, shelves of books with plots that would keep us entertained for hours if we could but read them. But the tombstones sometimes offer clues about the tales hidden in the graves they mark.

Over in Schuylkill County, for example, on the south side of Tumbling Run Mountain, a single headstone sits alone in that lonely and god-forsaken wildwood. Today, its inscription is indecipherable, but records show it once read: Nathan Webb, hunter.[1]

The Webb family were early settlers in Tumbling Run Valley, so possibly the man buried in that lonely grave on Tumbling Run Mountain is of that same family. Maybe he was killed in a hunting accident here, given the reference to "hunter," but why he was buried on the mountain rather than in a family plot makes this burial so mysterious.

There is another marker that leaves little doubt about why it's there but does not sit on a gravesite. It is instead a cenotaph, or monument, that honors the young woman whose remains lie in the cemetery at Keewaydin in Clearfield County.

The cenotaph is along Route 879 between the villages of Snow Shoe and Karthaus in northeastern Clearfield County, and, as it sits back off the highway and lies just inside a shaded woodland, the unobtrusive marker can be easily overlooked by passersby unless they've come to find it.

---

1. E. Z. Elliott, Blue Book of Schuylkill County, 448.

Clara Price's Grave

The notation on the marker "Clara Price Murdered 1889 by Alfred Andrews" preserves the memory of the beautiful young mountain maid whose life was so savagely taken from her on November 27, 1889, by ne'er-do-well Alfred Andrews on this very spot. He was apprehended and hanged for his crime, but that is a tale that lovers of a good murder mystery would appreciate. See the chapter titled "Ghosts of the Graveyard" in the author's *Pennsylvania Fireside Tales Volume VII* for a complete account of the incident.

An actual gravesite in the cemetery of a small country church in Centre County is not hard to miss because of the impressive statue that marks its spot. A true *Memento mori* of large proportions, it rivals many similar graveside statues found in European cemeteries. And anyone looking at it will be struck by its melancholy aspects. Closer inspection will reveal why the statue of the woman sitting on the tombstone has such a downhearted and mournful appearance.

Inscribed on that massive memorial are the epitaphs of five people: Cora A. Luse (died Jan. 16, 1862), Katie S. Luse (died Jan. 23, 1862), Father William Luse (died Jan. 26, 1862), Della M. Luse (died Jan. 30, 1892), and Mother Rosetta E. Luse (died 1912).

The Bereaved Mother's Memorial.

From the death dates of various family members, it can be seen that the mother of this family lost her husband and two daughters just days apart in the same month of the same year. Then, 30 years later, she lost a third daughter before she died 20 years later.

What caused so many deaths in such rapid succession in 1862 is not easily determined. But epidemics of smallpox, yellow fever, and typhoid fever took a heavy toll on mountain communities in the nineteenth century, so maybe one of those scourges is to blame.

Regardless of what happened, it's not surprising that the monument on the gravesite is a true *memento mori*, a reminder to everyone of what this

Epitaph of the Unknown Traveler.

The old country graveyard, showing the shadowy site of the "Unknown Traveler's unmarked grave, Rock Hill Cemetery, Linden Hall, Pennsylvania.

poor woman went through and a token to us all as to what may await us if our luck turns as bad as the mother buried here.

Another graveyard marker holds an inscription of a curious nature that drew my attention to it when I first ran across it in 2011. The marker lies inside a small country churchyard beside a former Methodist church in Linden Hall, Centre County. The names of those buried in the cemetery are on the marker, with one exception. On the lower right-hand corner are inscribed the words "Unknown Traveler."

Who the "Unknown Traveler" was is a mystery that will probably never be solved, as is the story behind his cause of death. Perhaps he was a hobo, or "bum," as they were termed back in the day, who found shelter in a local barn and died there at night. Regardless, the local god-fearing folks treated him respectfully and buried him in hallowed ground in an unmarked grave.

Of all the odd gravesites and markers I've ever run across, however, none rival the curious tombstone of red sandstone that sits on the slope of a mountain in Trough Creek State Park of Huntingdon County. The Paradise Cemetery is off the beaten path and, therefore, not often visited, but

Paradise Cemetery, Trough Creek State Park, Huntingdon County.

The "Indian Princess" tombstone, Paradise Cemetery, Huntingdon County.

those who do make the ascent to it by following the Kiln Road Creek Path up the mountain are no doubt surprised by the tombstone in question.[2]

Named for the Paradise Iron Furnace, built here in 1827 by Reuben Trexler and still seen in the park, the Paradise Cemetery seems to lull its visitors into a peaceful reverie as they stand in this land of twilight and shadow. The silence in this lonely spot is only broken by an occasional bird call or by the soughs of leaves moving in the soft mountain breezes, zephyrs which seem to deem it their eternal task to soothe the foliage that grows here and calm the spirits of the inhabitants that lie buried herein.

---

2. Pennsylvania Department of Conservation and Natural Resources, A Pennsylvania Recreational Guide for Trough Creek State Park, 2011.

But one denizen of this hallowed spot may never find that peace because their identity has been lost in the mists of time. Legend holds that she was an Indian princess, but history and tradition do not support that idea. Iron operations closed down in 1856, so the person buried here, judging from the 1895 date on the tombstone, was most likely a member of one of the families who were employees of the lumbering operations that followed.

Whoever they were, they evidently must have been much loved. The heart-shaped carving on the tombstone seems to indicate as much. There are also what appear to be two sets of initials (MF and IK?) engraved on the stone, so does that indicate that two people share this burial site? It only adds to the mystery that will most likely never be solved.

Yet another mystery awaits those who visit a gravesite that sits along the edge of a farmer's field in Polk Township of Jefferson County. The headstone here preserves the name of the person whose grave it marks, but the large boulder that towers over it holds the key to the mystery that unfolded around it.

This strange story begins with the life of one Richard Slyhoff, who died at the relatively young age of forty-three in 1867. Slyhoff lived a life of self-indulgence in what seemed to be an unending quest for pleasure. His main activities, to the disgust and displeasure of his neighbors, were whore-mongering, drinking, gambling, and avoiding the inside of a church, as he was never seen at any Sabbath service, even on the holiest days.

But despite it all, he had a long-suffering wife who bore him seven children, and as he grew older, those children and his sins must have begun to cause him to have second thoughts about his ill-spent life. Then as his death approached, he began to talk to anyone who would listen about his immortal soul and how it must be destined to spend eternity in the fiery pit.

He even was heard to muse about how he could somehow thwart the devil from carrying off his soul to that hellish abode. And one day, after noticing a large boulder on a slope near his residence, he devised a plan that seemed foolproof, given the size of the rock monolith.

Slyhoff reasoned that when the Day of Judgment came, earthquakes, thunderstorms, and other rumblings would cause the earth's entire surface to undulate and shake. This disruption, he decided, would cause that huge

Richard Slyhoff's Rock and grave, Jefferson County.

boulder to move down the slope on which it stood, but probably not more than a few feet.

Carrying his reasoning forward, Slyhoff thought that if he were to be buried just next to the rock, it would solve his problem. After all, when the earth shook and trembled on Judgment Day, the rock would slide downhill just a bit, seal his grave, and thus prevent the devil from getting his soul.

It was a pretty irrational and far-fetched idea, but when Slyhoff died, his friends honored his wishes. Working on their hands and knees, they picked away at the rocky ground just underneath the edge of the rock and eventually managed to dig a grave for the deceased. He was buried there

Richard Slyhoff's tombstone, Jefferson County.

with little ceremony and with many no doubt thinking, "good riddance to bad rubbish,'

And that would no doubt have been the end of the story had not one of the burial party noticed something quite strange upon returning some years later. Although Judgment Day had not yet come, the rock had indeed moved but had not moved downhill. It had moved uphill, as it continues to do to this day, seemingly defying all natural laws.[3] In doing so, it is perhaps the world's strongest *Memento Mori*. It is a reminder that, as mere mortals, we are destined to die and have no control over what happens to our soul once it leaves our body and moves on to the next world.

---

3. Joyce Holt, History of Polk Township, Jefferson County, 10.

Slyhoff's Rock and gravesite – a different perspective. I laid down on the grave to give a perspective as to how far the rock has moved uphill since Slyhoff's coffin was buried here. His body was in the opposite position to mine: his feet were under the rock and marked by the smaller upright stone, while his head was at the end marked by the headstone.

Footnote:

Richard Slyhoff's story is remarkably similar to that of one Meg Shelton, known to history as the "Witch of Woodplumpton" in Lancashire, England. Many dark tales were told about her; even today, people wonder why she was so defamed. But the evidence that she was regarded as a witch is there for all to see today. The inscription on the sign next to her grave reads as follows:

THE WITCH'S GRAVE
Beneath this stone lie the remains of Meg Shelton, alleged Witch of Woodplumpton, buried in 1705

The sign is enough to arouse the curiosity of most who see it, even those who are not otherwise historically inclined, but the huge boulder sitting on the gravesite is what makes people wonder. The reason it's there is a tale infused with the superstitious beliefs of the period in which Meg lived, and its very presence would no doubt appeal to the spirit of Richard Slyhoff.

Meg Shelton's grave, Woodplumpton Church graveyard, Lancashire, England.

The plaque on Meg Shelton's grave at Woodplumpton Church Graveyard. (Photo courtesy of David Ross, editor, Britain Express.)

Despite being convinced that she had used her unearthly powers as a witch to conceal herself while stealing from them and causing devilish mischief, Meg's neighbors buried her in the hallowed ground upon her death in 1705. That doesn't make sense if she had been thought to be a witch, but then things that must have changed people's minds began to happen.

It's related that on several occasions after she was buried, she dug herself out of her grave! At least the soil on the gravesite was seen to be freshly turned over on more than one occasion, and that was enough to convince the church fathers to exhume her body and rebury her vertically with her head downward and then seal her resting place with the huge boulder that sits there yet today!

Such burials were commonly done for those suspected of being in league with the devil. Archeologists call them "deviant" burials, and they've been found in other countries besides England. But in Meg Shelton's case, it was no doubt morbid curiosity seekers who dug her up more than once to look at the corpse of a supposed witch, and then it became a case of superstition overruling reason that led to this final abuse of her earthly remains.

People still come to view her grave today, but most no doubt walk away feeling a degree of sympathy for someone who was so unjustly accused when alive and whose body was so badly abused after being entombed.[4]

It is said that many of those same locals believe that should you walk around the stone over Meg Shelton's grave three times, you will be granted good luck. On visiting the churchyard, fresh flowers are often found on her grave. Woodplumpton photos courtesy of David Ross, editor of *Britain Express*.

> **LOCATIONS:**
>
> **Trough Creek State Park:** The Park is in Rothrock State Forest near Raystown Lake and the village of Entriken in Huntingdon County (DD GPS Coordinates: 40.3286879, -78.1313961). From Huntingdon in Huntingdon County, drive 16 miles south on Route 26, then near the village of Entriken, follow PA Route 994 east to the park entrance
>
> **Slyhoff's Rock:** The rock is on private property owned by Bill's Hide-A-Way Cottages, Brookville, Jefferson County, and close to Allegheny National Forest (DD GPS Coordinates: 41.16117, -79.08309). From Route 80, exit onto TR4005 (Richardsville Road) and then make a left-hand turn onto TR 484 (Dixon Road). In about 100 yards, turn right onto Firetower Road. Follow for several miles until you see Bill's Hide-A-Way Cottages on the left. The address is 2647 Firetower Road, Brookville, PA 15825. Slyhoff's Rock is on their property, which is private property.

---

4. https://flickeringlamps.com/2015/08/14/buried-under-a-boulder-the-grave-of-a-lancashire-witch/.

CHAPTER 8

PICTURE ROCKS

The name "Picture Rocks" must immediately evoke visions in many peoples' minds of colorful works of art painted upon a natural canvas of rocks. No doubt those mental pictures come from seeing the multi-colored images drawn today by disrespectful graffiti artists on railroad cars, retaining walls, and even (and this is the highest level of disrespect of all) natural rock formations. But the pictures on the rocks in Lycoming County have a far different provenance.

For one thing, the pictures on those rocks no longer exist. Time and the forces of nature had slowly eroded them away, having centuries to do so since they were placed there long before the first white settlers came into this same area.

Those later settlers found the artwork on the rocks and were amazed and intrigued by them. The crude images painted on the rock face posed a real mystery for them. They knew that the Indians had placed them there, but they had no idea why they did so or what message the drawings were meant to convey.

As can be expected, the pictures were an object of curiosity for decades, but the message they held was never discovered, and any attempt to discover it vanished as the pictures crumbled away. Moreover, it seems that no one ever thought to draw a picture of them before they disintegrated into the waters of Big Muncy Creek and were washed into the waters of the West Branch of the Susquehanna River and then out to sea.

Today the 200-foot high rock ledge where the pictures once appeared is still surrounded by high mountain peaks and rocky outcrops. A small park

The rock "canvas" at Picture Rocks, on which early Native Americans drew their strange symbols and motifs, and which later became the basis for the name of the rocks on which they were placed and also the name of the small town that grew up beside them.

and picnic area maintained by proud citizens of the town sits on the other side of the creek, as does the quaint little town itself, which was named for the Indians' artwork.

Although the Indian artist's pictures no longer adorn the rocks along the creek, nature provides its artistic touches from time to time, especially when the creek is high. Then, tiny rainbows dance amidst the mists and spray of the creek as it tumbles over the rocky creek bed in the sunlight. And also at nighttime when the moon casts a soft half-light over the cliff-side rocks, and fantastic shadowy patterns emerge and dance in the night wind's whispers. Such displays can be appreciated as much today as they undoubtedly were by the Indians who once passed through here.

The town's history has even more of a connection to those same Indians since archeologists have confirmed that the tiny village of Picture Rocks sits on the site of a favorite camping place for a tribe of Muncy Indians that once made this area their home. The nearby town of Muncy is named after them, and the many arrowheads, beads, and other relics they left behind and which have been found at Picture Rocks confirm their presence in years past, as do the "pictures" they drew on the rocks.[1]

Perhaps the symbols that could once be seen on the rocks, and which were evidence of the Indian's artwork, were identical to those that once were preserved on a drawing made by Captain Eastman in 1853 when he found similar strange markings on a large boulder known as Indian God Rock on the banks of the Allegheny River near present-day Franklin, Venango County.[2]

Indian God Rock is still there, but the strange symbols that once decorated it have been largely obliterated, like those at Picture Rocks in Lycoming County, by vandalism, flood waters, and winter freeze/thaw cycles. The sarsen was placed on the National Register of Historic Places in 1984 after experts at the Carnegie Museum of Natural History determined that the "petroglyphs," or "rock symbols," were made between A. D. 1200 and A. D. 1750 by Algonkian Indian shamans for religious purposes. They represent some of the earliest petroglyphs discovered by the first settlers in the region.

Those same settlers noted how much the Indians revered the rock and its decorations and thus dubbed it "Indian God Rock." Decades later, as steamboats plying the river passed by the landmark, the steamboat captains would shout out "Indian God Rock," and passengers would crowd to that side of the boat to see it.[3]

Despite the absence of the Indians' drawings on the cliffs at Picture Rocks

The Picture Rocks Petroglyphs? Perhaps the symbols above are identical to those that once appeared on Lycoming County's Picture Rocks since they closely resemble those once found on a large boulder known as Indian God Rock on the banks of the Allegheny River near present-day Franklin, Venango County. From the drawing made in 1853 by Captain Eastman.

---

1. John F. Meginness, History of Lycoming County, 515.
2. Donald A. Cadzow, "Safe Harbor Report No. 1," Penna. Historical Commission, Harrisburg, 1934.
3. http://www.venango.pa-roots.com/indiangodrock1.html.

"Seein' Things at Night." Local artist John Wesley Little's fanciful depiction of the Picture Rocks in Lycoming County. (Photo courtesy of the Pennsylvania State Archives. MG 213 Postcard Collection, ca. 1880–1974.)

today, there is at least one physical reminder of their presence here, at least if local legend can be trusted. This reminder is a gravesite hidden away in a woodland that sits just above the cliffs at Picture Rocks.

This little-visited spot is on private property and should be respected as such. The current owner was gracious enough to allow us to visit it when we inquired about it in 2023, but he claimed he did not even know where it was or anything about it. Had it not been for the local lady escorting us to the spot, we would never have found it.

Such is the unrelenting determination of time to erase the memories of the past if we do not try to preserve them. But this place of internment is

Picture Rocks

Near the same spot where artist John Wesley Little drew inspiration for his "Seein' Things at Night" drawing.

Close-up view of the "Indian Head" on Picture Rocks, as it appears today and the exact place where John Wesley Little, internationally-famed landscape artist from Picture Rocks, must have sat to draw the image on the "Seein' things at night" postcard. Little died in 1923 at age 57. His paintings are much sought after today.

The Indian Grave. Very few people know about it today, nor where to find it. Nestled along a little-traveled byway on the mountain above Picture Rocks, the gravesite is a quiet and peaceful place and an ideal spot for an internment.

still visible, and there are those still alive who recall previous owners maintaining the gravesite with meticulous care, even going so far as marking it with a plaque engraved with the legend about those buried here. The plaque is no longer there, its current whereabouts unknown, but rocks still encircle the grave, and the legend is still recalled by the older generation of valley residents, who still marvel at the story and wonder how true it might be.

According to the local legend, two people are buried here, and both are Native Americans. Their tale of woe is a love story that no doubt has been often experienced by star-crossed lovers over the ages, so that common theme may give some credence to the tale of the lovers buried in this lonely spot.

The names of the Indians have been lost to the ages, but here supposedly lie a local Indian chief and his maid. Both were smitten with the other when still young and alive, and they had pledged their undying love for all eternity. However, a fatal illness overcame the beautiful maiden, and so before she and her dusky prince could start their lives together, she passed into that same eternity.

The loss was too great for the Indian chief, and he could not recover from the loss of this true love. Perhaps the same sickness had claimed his sweetheart or something even more deadly, but whatever it was, it swiftly claimed him.

Knowing how deeply he and his maid had loved one another, his fellow tribesmen kindly interred them in the same grave, thus insuring that their remains, at least, would be together for as long as the sun shone upon them. The spot is peaceful today, with sun-dappled woods surrounding it.[4]

> **LOCATION:** The Picture Rocks cliff face is across Big Muncy Creek in the town of Picture Rocks in Lycoming County. It seems fitting that nature marked this spot with the Indian face, the place where Indian campfires once burned and where they drew or carved their petroglyphs on the rocks that still bear the name of those same pictures (DD GPS Coordinates: 41.279803, -76.7080114). Follow 220 East from Williamsport and 405/220 North through Hughsville to Picture Rocks. Turn right on Water Street in Picture Rocks and pull into the small Picture Rocks parklet on the left and across from the cliff face.

---

4. Ethel M. Cruse, History and Pictures of Picture Rocks, Penna., self-published pamphlet written for the Lycoming County Historical Society.

CHAPTER 9

BOXCAR ROCKS

One of Pennsylvania's most spectacular natural landmarks has to be a massive rock face in Cold Spring Township, Lebanon County, known as "Boxcar Rocks." Also known to locals as "High Rocks" or the "Chinese Wall," this spectacular rock formation resembles, as the name implies, railroad boxcars piled one on top of the other. The descriptive appellation came from a local county politician, who, in the 1940s, said they resembled a "railroad wreck of boxcars." The name appealed to the public, so the rocks have been known as Boxcar Rocks ever since.

Located on State Game Land 211 near Jonestown in Lebanon County, it is a favorite spot for rock climbing enthusiasts and is considered by them, and by many others, to be one of the most impressive rock "cities" in the state. Situated on the narrow knife-edge-sharp ridge line of Sharpe Mountain, the rocks are interspersed with veins of quartzite deposits which set them apart even more.

Said to be remnants of receding glaciers during the Ice Age, their origin was not of concern to the ever-practical Native Americans, who, historians tell us, used the alcoves in the rocks as camping nooks and the summits of the rocks as good places to set roaring fires ablaze to send smoke signals to their hunting parties in the nearby Blue Mountains.[1]

---

1. Joshua Groh, "Boxcar Rocks are one of Lebanon's best hiking spots," 10/25/2020, found at www.Lebtown.com. Information also found at www.stonyvalley.com/boxcar.

A bird's eye view of the "Chinese Wall." (Photo courtesy of Joe Forte.)

An intrepid climber scaling the "Chinese Wall." (Photo courtesy of Joe Forte.)

A "boxcar" at Boxcar Rocks.

Another "boxcar" at Boxcar Rocks.

The author at the "whale's head," the most iconic boulder at Boxcar Rocks.(This is a photo-shopped version in order to hide the stark graffiti on some of the rocks. More disgusting evidence of the utter callousness of certain misguided and self-entitled despoilers.

LOCATION: Boxcar Rocks is in Cold Spring Township of Lebanon County (DD GPS Coordinates: 40.54680, -76.5261). From the borough of Dauphin in Dauphin County, follow Route 225 North to its intersection with Clarks Valley Road (Route 325) off to the right. Turn right onto Route 325 and head northeast. Follow Route 325 for about 50 miles until you come to an intersection with Greenwood Road on the left and Gold Mine Road off to the right. Turn right onto Gold Mine Road and follow it until you navigate a series of hairpin turns. Shortly after the hairpins, look for a large gated road and parking area on the left, on top of Sharp Mountain, and pull into it. You've gone too far if you reach the top of the next mountain (Second Mountain). We found that the online instructions for this pullover were incorrect and misleading. The correct gated pullover was hard to identify.

If hiking, walk past the metal gate and follow the road. It veers off to the right, and in about ½ mile, look for a well-worn hiking path off to the right. Follow this path through pine woods a short distance and look for a Boxcar Rocks sign. Rocks are within view.

CHAPTER 10

WARRIORS' MARK

Mountains are magical in many ways, with the blossoming of wildflowers in the spring, the blazing dazzling colors in the fall, and the sparkling of ice and snow in the winter making them seem even more so. But the colorful tales these ancient hills embrace enhance their mystical appeal, making them more alluring and enticing to romance and mystery lovers. But mysteries often surround such tales and the places of which they tell since their true history has been lost over time. In this chapter, I'd like to hold forth one such example and provide evidence to show it may have some truth behind it after all.

The subject of this particular tale was once a revered landmark in a secluded forest glen near the quaintly-named village of Warriors Mark in Huntingdon County. Founded in 1768, this small mountain community is located to the south of the nearby Bald Eagle Mountains and just a few miles west of picturesque Half-Moon Valley in Centre County. Historians have agreed that that valley's name came from the many half-moon blazes on trees the early settlers found when they first came here, which they determined had been carved there by the Indians.

Historian John Blair Linn writes, "The name Half-Moon is popularly supposed to have been applied to the township and valley because of the rude representations of half-moons found by the early settlers upon trees, marking the course of an Indian trail passing through the valley. It is held that these signs and others illustrative of the various phases of the moon were fixed upon trees by bodies of wandering Indians to indicate to such of their tribe as might follow them that they had encamped at such places at certain periods of the moon's changes."[1]

Other early Huntingdon County historians like J. Simpson Africa and Albert Rung mention these "warriors' marks" in their area histories and offer them as the most likely explanation as to why that name was chosen for the Huntingdon County town. These scholars supported their theory by noting that trees near the town of Warriors Mark once displayed other Indian carvings, meanings of which were equally mysterious and, just like the carvings on the trees in Half-moon Valley, must have been the basis for the town's name.

However, older residents of the area maintain to this day that neither Africa nor Rung got it right, that there is another explanation as to which warriors mark was the one from which the town took its unusual name. The historians' explanations, they said, did not coincide with the stories they had heard their grandparents tell, and those tales, they claimed, had physical evidence to support them.

The descendants of these earliest settlers noted that their ancestors claimed to have no idea as to what the significance of the tree carvings was to the Indians, and so they could never determine their true meaning. But then they would tell of another tree still standing that held the original "warriors mark." They would further claim that the "mark," a large flat stone inserted into an indentation on the tree, was still there, and it was of great importance to the Native Americans who once made this valley their home and used that very "mark" for target practice.

The historians' contention that Native Americans left their marks on trees in Half-Moon Valley is consistent with other accounts of Indian carvings found on trees in central Pennsylvania. In a newspaper article appearing in the *Centre Democrat* of Bellefonte dated July 11, 1896, the writer (no name given) recalled that "It may be worthy of notice that there was an Indian path across [Penns] Valley, parts of which are visible in this day, and were seen by the writer. It is known to have terminated at a point opposite Pine Creek on the West Branch where there used to be an Indian graveyard."

---

1. John Blair Linn, History of Centre and Clinton Counties Pa., 308.

"Sioux Tribal Ceremony, Dakota Territory, 1866." From a sketch by C. Moellman. Appeared on page 324 of Frank Leslie's Illustrated Newspaper, February 10, 1866. Perhaps a good illustration of the Indian ceremonies at the Indian oaks near Warriors Mark!

[Current stream maps show no creek denoted as Pine Creek flowing into the West Branch; the Indian path to which the writer must have been referring is the Penns Creek Path (also known by the Indian name of Karoondinha Path), and the creek he must have had in mind is Penns Creek; Pine Creek flows into Penns Creek at the village of Woodward in Penns Valley, Centre County, and Penns Creek flows eastward to the West Branch].[2]

"At the foot of Nittany Mountain," he continued, "north of George Brungart's farm, there was fitted through a small tree a polished stone 18 or 20 inches long and about 3 inches in diameter. It probably served as a 'guideboard' to the path. On top of Nittany Mountain, the figure of a turkey was carved upon a tree near the path, and various marks on trees and rocks were still to be seen until a few years ago. The path was steeply worn in some places, which shows that it was used frequently."[3]

This description supports both the contention that Native Americans fashioned half-moon carvings on trees in Half-Moon Valley to serve as trail

---

2. Paul A. W. Wallace, Indian Paths of Pennsylvania, 126.
3. "Miles Township," newspaper article appearing in the Centre Democrat, Bellefonte, Pa, 07/11/1896.

markers and also the idea that they could have placed a stone on a mighty oak to use as a true warriors' mark. And, much to my chagrin, I missed seeing that same stone by about ten years.

Those who like to explore the back paths and little-traveled byways of the Pennsylvania countryside may already be familiar with state Route 350, which connects the villages of Spring Mount and Warriors Mark in Huntingdon County. The pretty little country highway skirts broad expanses of tilled fields and passes well-kept farms, taking a traveler back to a time when developments had not yet become the dominant feature of the countryside. Also figuring prominently in the scenery, the dark expanse of Tussey Mountain to the south and the well-wooded slopes of Bald Eagle Ridge to the north are other scenic attractions that can draw a traveler's attention away from other, less noticeable points of interest along the way, like the name of another country road that cuts off the state road and leads to points east.

Indian Tree Lane may not be noticed by most people who travel through here for the first time. There is a street sign with the name Indian Tree Lane displayed upon it at the mouth of the road, but many people probably think it's just another common highway sign and don't even give it a second glance. However, by ignoring the byway, they are missing the opportunity to see an old landmark that is a remarkable survivor of a much earlier day.

The first tendency many alert Route 350 travelers might have upon seeing the sign for Indian Tree Lane is to head east on this road to seek out the old tree that the road must be named after. However, the tree in question sits back in the woods on the west side of Route 350, diagonally northwest of the entrance to Indian Tree Lane. But even if someone knows where to look, the old oak tree is not easily seen; unless winter is approaching and the higher bushes along the highway have been killed off by the onslaught of the cold frosts of late fall, and the trees here have been stripped of their colorful autumn leaves by those same wintry frosts.

But even when no longer protected from view by the leaves on the trees between it and the state road, the ancient oak may still be ignored by passersby because they think it looks just like any other old tree. However, if they knew the story behind the ancient forest monarch, they might stop

The Last Survivor. The remaining oak tree of the four original oaks that held the warriors' marks. It was still standing near the village of Spring Mount, Huntingdon County, when I took this picture in June of 2018.

and try to see it from a closer vantage point; try to determine for themselves if the evidence supports what locals say is the true origin of the name Warriors Mark.

According to those local accounts, the Route 350 oak is the last standing survivor of four oaks that once stood at this spot, each tree forming the corner of a rectangular area where Indians once camped. In this area, locals believe that the Indians often danced around their campfires and rehearsed their warrior games, one of which was target practice.

And the targets, the "warriors' marks," at which they used to throw their tomahawks, it was widely accepted, were stones lodged in a hollow

The Warriors' Mark. Close-up of the last oak of the four original oaks that held the warriors' marks. The triangular indentation where the rock target was placed is seen near the top of the picture.

spot in each of the four oaks. Three of the four oaks are gone, but until about ten years ago, an original warriors' mark stone could still be seen lodged in a hollow area of the remaining oak.

But the old stone relic is gone now, too, surreptitiously carried off without permission, much to the chagrin of locals, to an Indian museum in the mid-west. There the historic stone can most likely still be seen today, which, along with the still-living oak tree used to hold the warriors' marks, proves that the past is never really that far away.[4]

---

4. Wilson Catherman, (born 1929) and interviewed by the author December 31, 1999.

CHAPTER 11

VAMPIRE ROCK

Mountains are enchanting places. Just letting the eyes rest upon their dark blue profiles is soothing to the mind and the spirit. But they can also intimidate those traveling along a lonesome mountain highway at night. With dense forests lining both sides of the roadway, the darkness seems impenetrable, especially when, for miles on end, no lights would indicate residences that may be otherwise hidden in those same woods. At such times the traveler may begin to hope that their car does not decide to die and leave them stranded. With no cell phone service and little traffic, it could be a long night before help can be found.

At that time, we might start to imagine dangers that lurk in the darkness and recall stories of ghosts, witches, and other supernatural entities that we've heard or read about in the past, which we enjoyed for their colorful descriptions and impossible scenarios. Nonetheless, under less pleasant circumstances, we may start to wonder about a hidden world that may be indiscernible by our human senses, a dimension that lies beyond our comprehension.

It is then, when stranded all alone along a little-traveled and unpopulated highway at night, or when disoriented and wandering in a dark and misty forest as chilly fall winds roar through giant pine trees or moan around the eves of a deserted haunted homestead sitting in a lonesome hollow, that we are more susceptible to imaginings that we would otherwise dismiss as fanciful.

Fanciful thoughts are bound to arise when standing under the gnarled branches of forest monarchs, with twisted tree roots clawing up from the ground upon which we stand. Unusual burls protruding from trunks of those same trees, splashes of vivid mushrooms of all shapes and colors decorating the landscape, and the murmurs and mists of swiftly flowing mountain streams also encourage such notions. And the chilling thoughts do bubble up, even though we know that science has overridden the idea that witches could work in league with the devil to wreak havoc on humankind and that ghosts still promenade at night to bathe in the glow of our electric lights.

But among those imaginary demons of the night, the vampire has to be one of the most well-known and improbable entities featured in this same paranormal domain. This bloodthirsty monster has been a popular subject in the folkloric cultures of various European countries since the dawn of storytelling in Medieval Europe, with each country assigning its name to the beast.

Hence there was the *Strigoi* which lurked in the darkest recesses of the Carpathian Mountains of Romania; the Shtriga, which inhabited the much-feared Accursed Mountains of Albania; the V*rykolakas* in Greece, where travelers avoided the island of Santorini, or "Island of the Vampires"; and the *Nachzeher* of Germany which cast a sense of dread and foreboding in those traveling through the Harz Mountains, the Kirchlengern Forest, or parts of the Black Forest.[1]

The idea of the existence of such a creature was strengthened and sensationalized by English writer John Polidori in his 1819 fictional novel titled *The Vampyre* and also by Bram Stoker in his 1897 fictional work titled *Dracula*. As a result, the name "vampire" became the most popular title used to refer to these blood-sucking phantasms; it was an idea so powerful that it survived well into the twentieth century in some of the most isolated areas of the world.

I also found this true of superstitions and beliefs about witches and witchcraft when I began collecting the legends and folktales of the Pennsylvania mountains in 1970. Much to my surprise, I could, even at that late date, still talk to people who subscribed to the idea that there were witches of the olden days still conjuring up their evil spells, old crones who could ride broomsticks and turn themselves into black cats. It showed how

---

1. Various scholarly attributions under the Wikipedia entry for "Vampire."

deeply entrenched those old concepts were and how strongly they clung to some segments of the populace.

Such notions were transplants from Medieval Europe, proving that ideas such as these seem to possess ageless impunity when traveling down through the mists of time for centuries. And, as might be expected, the belief in vampires also came along for the ride.

Legendary accounts of vampires in Pennsylvania seem to be scarce, however, never reaching the same level of popularity as that of ghosts and witches. But there was one that came close and was well-known in Northumberland County: the tale of the Werewolf of Line Mountain. Rather than detail that account, I refer readers to chapter 14 in *Volume 6* of the author's *Pennsylvania Fireside Tales* titled "A Line Mountain Werewolf Tale."

That much-maligned yet prolific collector and author of such stories, Henry W. Shoemaker, did record several vampire/werewolf stories he claimed he heard from the people he interviewed in the central Pennsylvania mountains in the first decade of the twentieth century (see "The Werewolf in Pennsylvania" in the Summer 1951 issue of the *New York Folklore Quarterly*, and "Another Werewolf" in the Winter 1951 issue of that same publication).

In addition, several of Henry Shoemaker's incomplete and unpublished stories are in the Lycoming County Historical Society archives in Williamsport. In one of those folders is a remarkable, apparently unfinished story titled "How Zora Machamer Eluded the Vampire of Rauch's Gap."

Shoemaker was noted for embellishing and even inventing such stories and also for naively accepting as fact the stories related to him by local tellers of tall tales. In this case, Shoemaker claims that the Rauch's Gap vampire story was told to him by one S. Jim Sheasley, "the Sage of Mt. Zion."[2]

Locals I interviewed in that same area and who had known Mr. Sheasley as a teller of tales had a dim view of his veracity. When asking them about such highly improbable local tales like that of the "Dancing Cupboard of Pine Mountain" (see chapter 11 titled "Dark Side of the Mountains" in the author's *Pennsylvania Fireside Tales Volume 7* for details), their first response was that "ooh, that probably came from old Jim Sheasley."

---

2. Appeared in the Journal of the Lycoming County Historical Society, Volume XXII, Number 2, Fall 1985, page 6.

So with this cautionary warning in place, we can summarize/paraphrase Shoemaker's Rauch's Gap vampire story as follows:

"It was a relief to the pioneers in Nippenose Valley, situated in Clinton and Lycoming Counties when news came that the alleged descendants of good old chief Nippenuce had left their stronghold in Rauch's Gap, near Ravensburg," so begins Shoemaker's treatise.

This small band of Indians, according to Shoemaker, had settled on a high rock formation by Rauch's Creek but were considered squatters by their pioneer neighbors. The Indians' neighbors did nothing to evict the trespassers for fear of stirring up Indian troubles, which had finally subsided only years before. Thus it was that the Indians were largely ignored, except for a few young small game hunters who were drawn to the Indian camp by the presence of an attractive young white woman who the Indians said was the adopted daughter of the chief.

The story of her adoption sounded too implausible to the area's settlers, who agreed that she instead must have been captured when very young and raised by her Indian captors until she had become, in all respects, an Indian in her looks and her nature. But she went by the English name of Zora Machamer and had the physical features of a beautiful white woman. And with all the coyness of refined beauty, she was always shy and retiring, expressing no desire to get to know any of the young bucks who tried to draw her into conversations.

But as time wore on, the would-be suitors noticed that Zora became increasingly emaciated, looking pale as death and wasting away. Then as her illness worsened, her superstitious Indian companions, recalling the tribal legends of vampires and cannibal ghosts, decided it would be too dangerous to stay with her at night, as it was then that these evil spirits would creep into cabins and suck the blood and flesh of their victims.

The Indians also recalled that at night the spirits were invisible, but in the daytime, these evil entities took the form of ravens or "Raven-mockers," as the Indians called them, owing to their raucous, discordant cries. The Indians were reminded of the old legends daily since the cliffs along the gap were the favorite nesting spots of many ravens, whose cries constantly echoed across the waters of the creek. In fact, there were so many ravens that the Indians became convinced that at least one of them had to be the cause of Zora's illness.

Then as Zora's condition worsened, her companions decided they needed to abandon her. Although it was inhumane, they knew that once the Raven-mocker had finished with her, it would move on to another member of the tribe to satisfy its lust for blood. Thus, one day, the settlers noticed that the Indians had suddenly left the area, not expecting that the ravens in the gap were responsible for their rapid departure.

Several days later, a couple of the young fox hunters who had previously admired Zora found her dying in the cabin where the Indians had abandoned her. Although badly dehydrated and covered with festering sores and tick and flea bites, Zora was nursed back to health by a local family who had no illusions about vampires and correctly assumed she was suffering from a serious illness like ones described in those days as "consumption" and "dropsy."

Shoemaker finishes his tale by stating that after regaining her health Zora eventually married a local lad and had children with him. "It is said," Shoemaker concludes, with his typical romantic flourish and in a fitting way to end a lurid story about vampires, "that their blood still exists in the beautiful Valley of Nippenose."

There can be no doubt as to the presence of ravens in great numbers at Ravensburg at an earlier time. As State Forest Ranger Edward B. Wentzel at Rauchtown wrote in July of 1923, "The Ravens at Rauch's Gap have been much in evidence this spring, rearing about eight young ones. They are almost always circling in the air, and it was an interesting sight to watch the old birds on their nests on top of the rocks."[3]

The ravens must have also lent an air of mystery to this place, especially at night when their weird cries pierced the silence of the forest. As George B. Stover of Stover's in Brush Valley noted in 1923, "Ravens are still here and nest on the point of the mountain beyond the head of Elk Creek. They fly backwards and forwards, and at nightfall, their croaking on the winds sounds so very odd to strangers, so different from that of a crow."

So Henry Shoemaker's highly-embellished vampire fantasy has some slight basis, in fact, but it is typical of his penchant for creating stories of this ilk, apparently, for the sole purpose of trying to instill an appreciation

---

3. Dorothy E. Shultz, synopsis of Henry W. Shoemaker letters and unpublished stories found in a box donated to the Society, Journal of the Lycoming County Historical Society, Volume XVI, No. 1 Spring 1980, p. 8.

for his beloved Pennsylvania mountains in others, with the hope it would lead to conservation efforts to preserve them for future generations. Therefore, his Rauch's Gap vampire story can be considered typical of others told for entertainment, with listeners often aware that they were of dubious authenticity.

One 86-year-old gentleman I interviewed back in 1983 recalled how he and other "old-timers" gathered around a pot-bellied stove in an old country store in Centre County every night to swap stories and exchange gossip.

"All those old fellas lied," he recalled, and such were the exaggerations in some of the reports, he noted, that one of those aged gentlemen once started the evening proceedings by asking, "Well, who's gonna tell the biggest lie tonight!"[4]

One might very well regard Shoemaker's vampire tale in the same way, but despite its fantastic elements, this tale, as with other seemingly "tall tales," may have some elements of truth behind it. On the other hand, after talking with locals, researching various volumes on the history of the West Branch and that of the counties of Clinton and Lycoming, and reading Donehoo's *Indian Villages and Place Name in Pennsylvania*, I could find no corroboration that Native Americans had a camp along the banks of Rauchtown Creek, which has carved a steep-walled gorge through the side of a nearby mountain.

That same gorge is the site of present-day Ravensburg State Park, and the name of that peak, Nippenose Mountain, is suggestive of Native American influences; however, that is debatable ground for some, who hold that the origin of the name is apocryphal and can no longer be determined with any certainty.

The origin of the name Nippenose for both the mountain and the nearby valley, according to historical sources that are considered reliable, was of Indian origin, with the name "Nippeno-wi" meaning "a warm and genial summerlike place." However, local accounts aver that the name was derived from an old Indian who lingered in the valley long after whites had settled it.

---

4. Mingle, Albert (born 1897 and interviewed by the author in 1983). See the chapter titled "Stretching It" in Pennsylvania Fireside Tales Volume 5, for more details.

John Wise of Oriole (1844–1914). The happy hermit of the Nippenose Valley who supported himself by hunting and trapping. He was the last professional hunter in the valley and no doubt could tell many tales of the olden days in Lycoming County. (Photo, taken in 1912, courtesy of Wayne O. Welshans.)

He stood out for that reason and because his nose had been "nipped" by frostbite and badly scarred from it, hence the nickname assigned to him. But a third explanation claims the limited access to the valley was the basis for the name. There was no way in or out without crossing over a mountain, and on the western edge, the gap through the mountain sort of nips part of it off, like a nip off someone's nose.[5]

So it seems that any evidence that Indians may have once resided at the base of the mountain with the unusual name has, like the origins of that name, been washed away by the currents of time. However, one unusual

---

5. Various scholarly attributions under the Wikipedia entry for "Nippenose Valley," and also in the History of Lycoming County, Pa. by John F. Meginness, page 593.

landmark near the site where they supposedly had their village can serve as a reminder of the Indians' presence in Nippenose Valley and a memoir of the weird vampire tale that purportedly was once told by early settlers along the waters of Rauchtown Gap.

It is a large, oddly-shaped rock pinnacle that imperiously towers over Rauchtown Creek just below. And since ravens had abandoned their former nests in the ledges at Ravensburg State Park, apparently driven off in 1933 when the road was cut through to establish the park, it seems appropriate to further memorialize their place in the area's legendary lore by assigning an appropriate name to that rock pillar. Therefore since it has never been assigned a name as far as I can determine, I've given it the name Vampire Rock as a nod to the story described above.

Vampire Rock. Profile of the vampire – a closer look reveals a forehead, eye, nose, and mouth. It determinately defies the ravages of time, as though its mission is to serve as a reminder to future generations of the unique qualities and legendary lore of this area)

CHAPTER 12

MORE OF THE SAME

I once read that the Appalachian Trail (AT) hikers have decided that Pennsylvania is where their boots "go to die." Apparently, extensive sections of the AT in Pennsylvania are so cluttered with jagged rocks that the sharp stones tear up hiking boots quite readily. But the wear and tear on hikers' boots is somewhat compensated for, I'm sure, by the marvelous sights along these same sections of the AT in Pennsylvania, landmarks already mentioned in this volume.

Nonetheless, there are other landmarks that I have discovered that deserve some attention as well. I've managed to get to most of them, but not all, and so many remain on my "bucket list," along with other places that could have also been visited. I am overwhelmed by how many of them there are. It seemed like I kept finding new ones when researching ones I'd already discovered, and I'm sure readers know of many themselves.

This richness of subject matter finally persuaded me to get this book to my publisher in a timely fashion; I would have to rely on others to provide high-resolution images of those places if I could not get to them myself before this book went to press. I also was satisfied that the book already seemed to include much of the "cream of the crop," as it were, and so these other places will perhaps have to wait. The information about each one that follows was found on various Internet sites; photos were taken by the author unless otherwise noted.

Whaleback Rock, as viewed to the southwest. The people on top give an idea of scale. (Photo by Gary Fleeger, courtesy of the Pennsylvania Geological Survey. Photo appeared in their Trail of Geology 16-110 publication under the title "Outstanding Geologic Feature of Pennsylvania – Whaleback, Northumberland County," by Stuart O. Reese.)

Whaleback Rock

While not as spectacular as some of the other rock formations heretofore mentioned, these huge rocks are heralded by geologists as one of the most impressive geological wonders in the eastern United States and possibly one of the best examples of "folded rock" structures in the entire United States. Pennsylvania has therefore designated them as an official Heritage Geology site, and as such, they serve as a natural classroom for geological studies of the forces that once molded our planet.

The seven-acre site is on the Bear Valley strip mine lands near Shamokin in Northumberland County. The size of the folds here is enough to make them unique, but it is their resemblance to the scarred back of an enormous sperm whale, with huge ironstone concretions resembling giant warts, that also make these dark gray rocks so spectacular. The rocks are on private land, but the Reading Anthracite Company of Pottsville sells admission tickets to get viewing access.

Monument Rock

Single rock pillars are always impressive, especially when over ten feet tall and fifteen to twenty feet high. Monument Rock along the Standing Stone

Whaleback Rock – a closer view. (Photo courtesy of the Pennsylvania Geological Survey.)

Monument Rock, along the Standing Stone Trail in Franklin County.

Monument Rock – a closer view

Trail in Franklin County is one such monolith. It is so unique that the Standing Stone Trail Club has adopted it as its club emblem. Some say it is this rock alone for which the Standing Stone Trail is named. The fact that it requires a mile-and-a-half uphill hike on a side trail to see it has no doubt protected it from graffiti-prone vandals who seem to take a fiendish delight in spoiling such natural wonders for everyone else.

Its location at the top of a boulder field of jagged rocks and the fact that it's virtually hidden in a canopy of surrounding trees cause it to be "un-photogenic," but it is nonetheless a conspicuous natural wonder to be enjoyed by those who make an effort to gaze upon it. Here too, can be seen the vertical sandstone walls along the ridge line, which lend their name to the trail, and interspersed among and around them are gigantic blocks of

A view of Chickies Rock. (Photo courtesy of Bruce E. Hengst Sr.)

gleaming sandstone that look like they could be the playthings of giants that once scattered them there.

Chickies Rock

As an extension of the Hallam Hills, this rock formation lies next to a wide water gap cut by the mighty Susquehanna River as it flows to the Chesapeake Bay in the south. Located in Chickies Rock County Park between the Lancaster County boroughs of Columbia and Marietta, its name comes from the American Indian word "Chiquesalunga," meaning "place of the crayfish."

Famous for being an observation point used by Union soldiers to observe Confederate troop movements during the Civil War, today, it still offers commanding views of York County across the river and of surrounding Lancaster County farmlands.

The rocks are an impressive quartzite outcropping towering 100 feet above the river and having a unique configuration. This particular type of geologic formation, a ridge-shaped fold of stratified rocks which slope downward from the crest, is thought by some to be the largest exposed anticline on the east coast.

With its Indian associations, it's no surprise that there is also an Indian legend told about this spot. According to the legend, it was here that a local Indian maiden fell in love with a white settler, who was killed in a battle fought by warring tribes over the romance between the two. Distraught by his death, she committed suicide by throwing herself off the cliffs and onto the rocks below.

Frog Rock

As opposed as I am to the despoiling of natural rock formations by graffiti "artists," I think there is at least one such place that may be an exception to the rule, and only because it draws attention to a natural wonder that would otherwise be just another rock in a stream. The rock in question sits in Tionesta Creek, which runs along Route 666 between the villages of Mayburg and Kelletville in Forest County. What would otherwise look like an ordinary rock poking up from the creek bed, locals have painted its natural contours in such a way that it resembles the head of a gigantic frog.

Even with its painted face, the rock is not easy to see, and I found it's best spotted when leaves are off the trees.

The Stone Men

When traveling along Route 80 East two years ago, I began to see, near mile markers 112 and 113, collections of stones set off from the sides of the roadway that I had never noticed before. Slowing down the car, I took a closer look and was surprised when I realized that the stones were arranged to resemble robots or stone men. Despite subsequent inquiries, I could never determine who built them or why, and when looking for them last year, I

Iconic Frog Rock, Forest County.

One of the stone men along Route 80.

"Guardian" of the Fred Woods Trail, Elk County.

could no longer see them. Perhaps vandals knocked them down, or the artists removed them, but they did provide a bit of unique scenery for a time.

I subsequently found no other figures like this, but in my hikes, I was sometimes taken aback by stone "faces" staring down at me from rock ledges along the trail. Although distorted images of human faces, they nonetheless added a degree of mystery to the remote wilderness through which I was trekking.

The images required a stretch of the imagination to bring them into focus, and when finally seen, it was obvious that they were nothing more than a trick of the brain; a tendency for it to make sense of random patterns, often imagining them to be facial features in particular. It is a human tendency Psychologists call "pareidolia."

See the chapter titled "The Three Sisters" for one such "face" seen peeking out between two trees along the Standing Stone Trail in the Rocky Ridge Natural Area of Huntingdon County. Yet another haughtily peered down at us from a rock ledge while silently guarding the Fred Woods Trail in Elk County.

Chimney Rock

Located near Hollidaysburg in Blair County's Chimney Rocks Park, hikers will be treated to three scenic views. The lower one offers a beautiful overlook of the town of Hollidaysburg, and the two at higher elevations offer more views of Hollidaysburg with breathtaking panoramas of the Allegheny Mountains that extend off into the horizon. But the prime attraction here is the rock pinnacle known as Chimney Rock, the rock for which the park is named.

There were apparently two such pinnacles here at one time, as evidenced by the scene depicted on an old stereoscopic card (public domain image follows). The two people sitting on top of the pinnacles on the card may have been part of the R. A. Bonine Stereoscope Company's plan to create a more appealing image. Having them sit there would make for a more interesting stereoscopic view, and their perches would have also been a reminder of widely-circulated and well-known legendary claim about these natural wonders that were popular at the time.

Chimney Rock - a steroscopic view

Chimney Rock today. The Rock for which the park is named. (Photo courtesy of Deborah Felmey.)

The mythical assertion was that local Native American chiefs considered them good viewing towers; the sachems would climb up the pillars and sit contentedly atop them to get commanding views of their surrounding hunting grounds. The legend was once so prevalent, it is said, that for years older area residents when asked about Chimney Rock, would refer to the "Chief's Seat" on top.

The Split Rock.

The Split Rock, with the author standing in the split to show relative size of this natural wonder. It is located near Lake Harmony and the Split Rock Resort in the Pocono Mountains of Carbon County.

The Ringing Rocks. A portion of the large boulder field that can be seen at this unique spot, located in Ringing Rocks County Park, Bucks County.

Split Rock

This Carbon County natural wonder must have had some Native American legends associated with it at one time, but I've found none and queries to local historians uncovered none. Looking just like it had been cleaved cleanly in two by the hatchet of the Native Americans' Great Spirit in a fit of anger, it is an amazing work of nature.

Ringing Rocks

This unusual natural landmark stretches the imagination. Who would believe that the rocks in this place ring like bells when struck with a hammer? It seems unlikely, but it's true, and this fact has made it a site of both mystery and superstition.

Pennsylvania Dutchmen called boulder fields like this one in Bucks County "felsenmeer," or seas of rock. They also had a peculiar belief about the rocks in this "sea of rocks," owing to the ringing noise the stones make when hit with a hammer. It was supposed at this earlier time that the odd

Ringing the rocks at Ringing Rocks. The author hammering the rocks to hear them ring.

sound meant that the rocks were hollow, and a large cache of gold or silver hidden inside was the cause of the ringing tones. It was an Old-World idea, with similar stones near the Welsh village of Maenchochog once smashed to bits to find their hidden treasure and the "golden ringing stone" of Fole in Sweden meeting a similar fate. No treasure was found in either case.[1]

Failure to find such riches in the rocks would be no surprise to geologists, who have studied their composition and tried to unlock their secrets. Their scientific explanations are still somewhat controversial, seemingly

---

1. Information found at https://pabucketlist.com/exploring-the-scenic-overlooks-at-chimney-rocks-park-in-blair-county/.

leaving us with no choice but to hold the stones in the same wonderment that ancient peoples once regarded them.

Historians believe that Native Americans knew about the sonorous properties of the rocks here and regarded the place as having special spiritual significance since their shamans believed it was an ideal spot for communicating with their Great Spirit and other forest spirits. It is perhaps this Native American belief that reinforced yet another legendary account that early local settlers once held as the Gospel truth regarding the origin of the unusual boulders.

Like the Devil's Turnip Patch in Lycoming County (see the chapter titled "Infernal Evidence"), this place (and a similar one called the "Devil's Potato Patch" in Salford Township of Montgomery County) was regarded as an attempt by the devil to discourage farming and settlement in areas that could otherwise be used for such purposes. In the case of the Ringing Rocks, the legend that clings to this spot recalls that the devil, after stepping over the Delaware River near here, sat down and, in a fit of diabolical bullying, polluted this very place by depositing or evoking, the rocks now covering the area.[2]

We know today that the rocks were formed from existing on-site rock masses by extreme freeze-thaw weathering cycles during the glacial era that once terraformed the entire state. But regardless of its origins, it is arguably, due to the repeated references to it in travelogues and chroniclers of mysterious sites, one of the most, if not the most, famous ringing rock locations in this country, and, as such, is well worth a visit by those who want to explore odd and mysterious places in Pennsylvania.

---

2. "Ringing Rocks and Sonorous Stones," dated October 8, 2020, found at https://spookygeology.com/ringing rocks.

BIBLIOGRAPHY

Bartlett, John, *Familiar Quotations*, Little Brown & Co., Boston, Mass., 2019.
Burke, James P., *Pioneers of Second Fork*, AuthorHouse, Bloomington, In., 2009.
Burkett, Kenneth P., "A Rockshelter Burial in Northwestern Pennsylvania," *Pennsylvania Archeologist*, Vol. 47, 1977.
Cornplanter, Jesse J., *Legends of the Longhouse*, Ira J. Friedman, Port Washington, N. Y., 1963.
Elliott, Ella Zerbey, *Blue Book of Schuylkill County*, Republican Press, Pottsville, Pa. 1916.
Egle, William H., *History of the Counties of Dauphin and Lebanon in the Commonwealth of Pennsylvania*, Everts & Peck, Philadelphia, 1883.
Herbstritt, James T. and Love, David A, "Archeological Investigations of Split Rock Shelter, Horton Township, Elk County, Pa., *Pennsylvania Archeologist*, Vol. 45, 1975.
Ignoffo, Mary Jo, *Captive of the Labyrinth: Sarah L. Winchester, Heiress of the Rifle Fortune*, University of Missouri Press, Columbia, Mo., 2010.
Jones, Richard, *Haunted Britain and Ireland*, New Holland Publishers, London, 2003.
Skinner, Charles M., *Myths and Legends of Our Own Land*, J. B. Lippincott, Philadelphia, 1896.
Swaminathan, Nikhil, "Meadowcroft Rock Shelter," *Archeology*, Sept./Oct. 2014.
Toy, Sidney, *Castles—Their Construction and History*, W. Heineman, London, 1939.
Wallace, Paul A., *Indians in Pennsylvania*, Pennsylvania Historical Commission, Harrisburg, 1970.
Welshans, Wayne O., *A Nippenose Collection*, privately published anecdotes and photos, 1995.

ABOUT THE AUTHOR

JEFFREY R. FRAZIER was born and raised in Centre Hall, Centre County, where he says he grew up in a "Tom Sawyer sort of way", later graduating with a BS from Penn State in 1967, and then an MBA from Rider University in New Jersey in 1978. Some of the fondest memories of his boyhood include explorations of out-of-the-way spots in the mountains and accounts of the legends that seem to cling to them, and beginning in 1970 he began collecting those same kind of anecdotes  from all over the state; ranging from the Blue Mountains of Berks and Lehigh Counties, the South Mountains of Adams County, the "Black Forest" area of Potter and Tioga Counties, the Alleghenies of Clearfield and Blair Counties, and the other counties in the middle. He has compiled his vast collection of tales into a series titled *Pennsylvania Fireside Tales*. This volume is a continuation of his work, written in a format that the average reader can enjoy, especially those who love the green valleys and cloud-covered mountain peaks of Pennsylvania as much as he does.

www.ingramcontent.com/pod-product-compliance
Lightning Source LLC
LaVergne TN
LVHW011425080426
835512LV00005B/275